**SHE WAS A BRILLIANT
ANTHROPOLOGIST'S WIFE . . .
SHE WAS A PROUD INDIAN'S
MISTRESS . . .**

ENCOUNTER WITH AN ANGRY GOD

**One of the most compelling true love stories
a woman has ever written**

"Fascinating . . . an extraordinary love story
which . . . sheds light on the differences between
the Indian culture and the white."
—*Los Angeles Times*

"A frank, unsparing personal record . . . a strong
flavorsome piece of Americana . . . a hit!"
—*San Francisco Chronicle*

ENCOUNTER WITH AN ANGRY GOD

Recollections of My Life with John Peabody Harrington

CAROBETH LAIRD

Foreword by Harry Lawton
Decorations by Don Perceval

BALLANTINE BOOKS • NEW YORK

Library of Congress Catalog Card Number: 73-88700

ISBN 0-345-26075-9-175

This edition published by arrangement with the Malki Museum Press

Manufactured in the United States of America

First Ballantine Books Edition: May 1977

Give not, give not the yawning graves their plunder;
Save, save the lore, for future ages' joy;
The stories full of beauty and of wonder
The songs more pristine than the songs of Troy,
The ancient speech forever to be vanished—
Lore that tomorrow to the grave goes down!
All other thought from our horizon banished,
Let any sacrifice our labor crown.

—John Peabody Harrington

 **CONTENTS**

 **FOREWORD**

IN THE EARLY decades of the twentieth century, the first generation of university-trained anthropologists, most of them disciples of Franz Boas or Frederick W. Putnam, fanned out across the North American continent to record everything which could be learned about the rapidly dying cultures of the American Indian. Their fieldwork led them to wherever dispossessed Indian groups had been herded onto reservations or pushed into remote backwaters as they sought out those old people who remembered how life had been before the coming of the white man. Their ranks included men and women who would become the pantheon of a new disciplinary profession—Robert H. Lowie, Alfred Kroeber, Edward Sapir, Elsie Clews Parsons, Paul Radin, Leslie Spier, and others.

Among these pioneer researchers shaping a new body of knowledge was the linguist-ethnographer John Peabody Harrington—a man driven by genius and so obsessed with a zeal for recording data that he ignored the traditional routes to academic prestige, rejected all efforts to bring his name to public attention, and considered any activity which took him away from fieldwork with informants to be a waste of time. Not a line concerning Harrington's career or achievements can be found in the standard biographies of his period devoted to science and letters. Eccentric, a reclusive person with few intimate friends, intensely suspicious of colleagues who he feared might steal his data, Harrington became a legendary figure in anthropological circles during his lifetime—a subject of numerous bizarre anecdotes, many of which are probably apocryphal.

Beginning in 1915, Harrington worked as a field enthnologist for the Bureau of American Ethnology for almost forty years, laboring up to eighteen hours a day, gathering significant data on almost every aboriginal linguistic group in North America from the Abnaki to the Zuni. Although he published sporadically and usually only under pressure from his superiors—more than a hundred papers and several books and long monographs—most of this published research is confined to specialized papers no more than a few pages in length. So intent was Harrington on amassing more and more quantities of data that he never completed those grand syntheses he believed would make his reputation and to which he sometimes alluded in unguarded moments with colleagues.

Harrington's monument lies in the literally tons of meticulous field notes he shipped to the Bureau of American Ethnology. It is believed that no other anthropologist ever gathered such a staggering quantity of material in the field as did Harrington. His notes on the Chumash Indians alone filled sixty boxes. He left almost a thousand pages of notes on the Kitanemuk Serrano—about whom very little has been known up to now. Early in his career, the material Harrington was gathering flooded the confines of the Bureau archives. Later it engulfed the basement of the nearby Freer Gallery. Finally, two commercial warehouses had to be rented in Washington to keep up with Harrington's prolific data-gathering. Even after his death in 1961, caches of manuscripts kept turning up in warehouses and depositories around the country where Harrington had stored and absent-mindedly forgotten them. The wealth of information left by Harrington is already broadening or changing our knowledge about many Indian groups, and it has been barely tapped. Ironically, Harrington's growing reputation and the increasing awareness of the greatness of his achievements rests on the use by other scholars of those notes which he always feared others were seeking to get their hands on.

In an obituary published in *American Anthropologist* soon after Harrington's death, M. W. Stirling, former chief to the Bureau of American Ethnology, paid high tribute to Harrington's genius as a scholar, while noting that he had always been a "mystery man" to the majority of his colleagues. Harrington still remains an enigma. Those scholars currently working with his papers find only occasional and conflicting clues about the man himself. Even the nature of Harrington's relationships with his Indian informants is obscured by contradictions. The Indians who worked with him appear to have regarded him with great affection and amused indulgence toward his idiosyncracies. To his credit, Harrington demanded and got higher informant fees for them than most anthropologists paid in his time. However, there is on record in Harrington's papers a contract which a Chumash informant signed promising not to give data to anyone else. And there are some rather harsh accounts of Harrington obtaining material from Indian co-workers who regarded him as a friend, whom he then dropped abruptly. On the other hand, Harrington is known to have maintained contact with some informants for thirty years or more. There are also tales of Harrington giving assistance to sick or infirm Indians long after he had ceased working with them. Finally, Harrington was nursed during his last years by one of his Chumash informants.

Carobeth Laird's *Encounter with an Angry God* is an intensely personal reminiscence of the seven-year period in Harrington's life when she was married to him. It is a bittersweet and transcendent book, hauntingly evocative of a time now gone, a token chronicle of what it meant to be a fieldworker in the formative years of American anthropology. The author has been unsparing both to Harrington and herself, in her depiction of the failure of their marriage. The book is also a love story—one of the strangest and most compelling love stories I have ever read, but the reader should discover that for herself or himself.

I doubt that this book could have been written in any other manner than that which Carobeth Laird has chosen. As a scholar in her own right, Mrs. Laird is aware of the tradition which dictates that the most private aspects of a scientist's life be handled delicately even in reminiscences, while permitting the widest latitude in dealing with the lives of novelists, poets, politicians, and other public figures. With considerable courage, she has chosen the course of pure autobiography rather than confining herself to the restraints of convention. Any fuller or more impartial account of that complex and curious personality who was John Peabody Harrington must await an official biographer.

Because Harrington is still so little known outside of his profession, I have been asked by Mrs. Laird to supply some background information for the general reader on his life prior to their marriage and his subsequent career and accomplishments after their parting.

John Peabody Harrington was born in Waltham, Massachusetts, on April 29, 1884, the son of an attorney, Elliott A. Harrington, and Mary L. Peabody. While he was still a small child, the family moved to Santa Barbara, California. In 1902, Harrington entered Stanford University majoring in anthropology and classical languages and graduating at the head of his class. While attending summer school at the University of California at Berkeley in 1903, Harrington's interest in California Indian languages was stimulated by the teaching of A. L. Kroeber and Pliny Earle Goddard. His determination to devote his career to American Indian languages and ethnography was probably made at that time.

Two years of graduate study followed during 1905 and 1906 at the Universities of Leipzig and Berlin, although Harrington did not wait to obtain his doctorate, so possessed was he with getting back to the United States and commencing fieldwork. Toward the end of 1906, he accepted a job teaching modern languages at Santa Ana High School in Santa Ana, California. All of his summer vacations and spare time for the next three years were devoted to studying the Chumash, Mohave, and Yuma Indians, living with them in their own homes and working with them late into the night.

In the fall of 1908, Harrington spent several weeks at the home of Matilda Coxe Stevenson near Black Mesa. Mrs. Stevenson, who was working with the Zuni, Hopi, and other pueblo peoples and gathering artifacts for the National Museum, was impressed with Harrington and brought him to the attention of W. H. Holmes, then head of the Bureau of American Ethnology. Her support led to a temporary and eventually a permanent post as an ethnologist for the Bureau.

In 1909, Harrington secured a position under Edgar L. Hewett as ethnologist for the School of American Archeology at Santa Fe, which over the next few years focused his research on the linguistics and ethnology of the Indians of the Southwest, particularly those of the Shoshonean, Chumashan, and Yuman linguistic stocks. In 1910, under the joint auspices of the School of American Archeology and the Bureau of American Ethnology, Harrington made a study of the ethnogeography of the Tewa. Out of this research, he published his *Ethnobotany of the Tewa Indians* (1917), a classic work that was far in advance of its time because of Harrington's attention to Indian systems of plant classification.

In 1911, Harrington conducted research on the Mohave at Lincolnia, Arizona, where he also gathered ethnological materials for the U.S. National Museum. For a brief period from 1911 to 1912, he served as assistant curator for the Museum of New Mexico at Santa Fe. On February 20, 1915, he finally received

his permanent appointment as field ethnologist for the
Bureau of American Ethnology in Washington, D.C.,
a position he was to hold for almost forty years.

In the summer of 1915, prior to beginning his
Bureau assignment, Harrington taught summer school
at San Diego Normal School. It was there he met a
nineteen-year-old student, Carobeth Tucker, whom
he married the following year, apparently attracted to
her because she had "one of the best linguistic ears"
—as he once phrased it—that he had ever encountered. She divorced him in 1922 to marry George
Laird, a Chemehuevi informant with whom both she
and Harrington had worked. The story of Carobeth's
four years in the field with Harrington and why she
finally left him is the subject of this book.

Virtually all of Harrington's research during his almost life-long career with the Bureau of American
Ethnology was concentrated on ethnologic and linguistic studies with one notable and ambitious exception. In 1923, he excavated the Burton mound at Santa
Barbara in the territory of his favorite group—the
Chumash. This side-jaunt into archeology was handled
with the same thoroughness and concern for detail as
all of his work, and the results were published in the
44th Annual Report of the Bureau.

In one sense, Harrington lacked formal training for
linguistics, having come to it through classical languages
and having only minimal training alongside his contemporaries who entered the field from eastern universities. He never abandoned his own phonetic
orthography, and he was so engrossed in field work
that he was scarcely aware of the course of develop-
ment of linguistic ethnological methodology. The prim-
ary value of the materials he left, however, lies in the
phonetic accuracy with which he recorded them using
his own system.

M. W. Stirling observed that no linguist was ever
acquainted with so many American Indian languages
over so wide a territory as Harrington. He had a more

than superficial command of an amazing number of languages. An alphabetical list of those American languages on which he left at least several hundred pages of manuscript would include Abnaki, Achomawi, Apache, Arapaho, Aztec, and so on through Wintu, Yunka and Zuni. He was especially interested in Aztec, Maya, and Quechua and prepared three large monographs on these classical languages of the high culture areas.

"His phenomenal memory of detail regarding the languages he had studied constituted real genius" Stirling wrote in a memorial essay. "I was so intrigued by this ability, that I frequently tested him by suddenly asking him how such and such a word was spoken, for example, by the Kato of California. He would not only respond immediately with the word, but give a dissertation on its derivation and connection with related words in other groups."

Both organization and publication were major difficulties for Harrington, since once he had exhausted a subject he lost enthusiasm for it, although he continued to talk of lofty plans for its future completion. The sheer mass of data he collected, according to Thomas Blackburn, may explain Harrington's "seeming inability to achieve an overview in spite of the repeated attempts to do so that are attested to by the various rough drafts of manuscripts scattered throughout his papers." Harrington also had almost no sense of proportion once an idea occurred to him. He once begged M.W. Stirling to send him to South America so he could trace the original form of the word tobacco from the Carib.

Harrington's fear that other colleagues were lying in wait to steal or cannibalize his data resulted in a passion for secrecy about his work that verged on paranoia. Except in his earliest notes, he never referred to informants by name, concealing their identities by means of cryptic symbols or abbreviations. Although for the most part Harrington's code has been cracked by scholars since his death, a few informants remain unidentified. Harrington also tried to throw a cloak of secrecy over his field activities, letting his superiors know only as much as he wanted them to know. Once he left for the field, he might be "lost" for months. The story may be apocryphal, but it has been said that one of the few ways his superiors devised for determining his whereabouts was to withhold his paycheck. This may not always have worked, since Harrington also had a reputation for forgetting to cash checks. Harrington's unorthodox methods and distaste for bureaucracy kept him in continual trouble with Bureau administrators and government officials at higher levels.

Although not much interested in theory, believing that once all the facts had been collected theoretical implications would become clear, Harrington was one of the first to suggest relationships between North and South American Indian languages. In 1910, he also postulated a relationship between Kiowa and Tanoan, which modern research has since confirmed. Although he abandoned the doctorate at the start of his career, the quality of Harrington's research was so impressive that in 1934 he was awarded the honorary degree of Doctor of Science by the University of Southern California.

The many anecdotes about John Peabody Harrington serve to accentuate the riddle of his personality. There are those who saw him as a kindly, generous man, who despite shyness possessed considerable social charm. There are just as many others who viewed him as misanthropic, opportunistic, and willing to go to any lengths to obtain more data. He seems to have made an indelible impression on everyone with whom he came in contact. William Sturtevant tells the story of mentioning to a taxicab driver in Oklahoma a few years ago that he was from the Smithsonian Institution. The cab driver—who had given Harrington a ride once twenty years before——immediately asked Sturtevant if he knew him.

Since Harrington's death in 1961, improved access

to his notes and a growing awareness of their importance has resulted in the appearance of numerous papers and books based on various aspects of the data he collected. Among those American researchers who have recently drawn upon or who are currently engaged in work with Harrington materials are Geri Anderson, Ann Anderton, Richard Applegate, Lowell John Bean, Madison Beeler, Thomas Blackburn, William Bright, Catherine Callaghan, Steven Craig, George Grekoff, Mary Haas, Robert F. Heizer, Linda King, Katherine Klar, Margaret Langdon, Pamela Munro, and Philip Wilke. Undoubtedly, there will be many more as the Harrington materials become better known and the immense task of cataloguing them moves to completion.

When Carobeth Laird left Harrington, she also left the world of anthropology for almost fifty years. In her middle seventies, however, she began to work on the first full-length book about the Chemehuevi Indians, drawing upon the material she had acquired mostly through her marriage to George Laird. The existence of the manuscript for that book, titled *The Chemehuevis,* was discovered by Lowell John Bean of California State University at Hayward in the spring of 1972, when he learned Mrs. Laird was still alive and went to see her about some of the Harrington materials on which she had worked. Her book on the Chemehuevi is scheduled for publication by Malki Museum Press.

Since reentering the world of anthropology, Mrs. Laird has published articles in the *Journal of California Anthropology* and has commenced a new book dealing with Chemehuevi myth. She is also collaborating with fellow scholars who are working on the Chemehuevi. The interest of a number of new friends in her reminiscences about life with Harrington led to her decision to write *Encounter with an Angry God.*

Carobeth Laird turned her back on the "yawning graves" of Harrington's poem, deciding against the single-minded sacrifices needed to amass mountains of field notes. In 1962, Catherine Callaghan of Ohio State University was sorting through Harrington's effects in a warehouse in Washington D.C. Suddenly, she came across some dust-covered birds in a box. Identified by labels both in Latin and in some American Indian languages, these desiccated birds had been stored unnoticed without benefit of taxidermy for twenty to thirty years. "It was at that point" she says, "that I concluded that a balanced life is more important than a life devoted exclusively to scholarship." Other researchers who have wrestled with their own doubts about the demands of scholarship have confessed that while working with the Harrington papers they too have felt a sudden flash of insight leading them to the same conclusion.

Harry W. Lawton
Riverside, California

I Encounter With An Angry God

I GOT OFF the street car and walked across Cabrillo Bridge. My nerves crawled with excitement and my mind spun incoherent fantasies. I imagined myself to be terribly ignorant and unworthy—and at the same time capable of greatness.

For almost two years I had been bringing home from the public library musty, outdated, inconceivably dull, and mostly incomprehensible tomes on paleontology, anthropology, and related subjects. You see, in the short time since we left that small, dreary Texas town where I was born, I had discovered *Evolution,* I had discovered *Science,* I had come to believe that there were those who spent their lives in pursuit of absolute truth, and I wanted above everything to belong to that elite band. But I couldn't "go to college" because I had never finished high school. Eventually I had nerved myself to approach someone at San Diego Normal School and lay my problem before him, someone about whom I remember nothing except that he was kind, reassuring, and practical. He advised me that a feasible first step would be to-enroll in the Summer School soon to open in Balboa Park. Therefore, on a bright morning in June, sweet with seabreeze and the scent of growing things, I walked across that impressive bridge (whence more than a few sad souls throughout the coming years would leap to their deaths) and on into the magnificent California Quadrangle and the beginning of a new life.

I must have been enrolled in a course in algebra, because it was in mathematics that I was most deficient. I must also have had a course in something, probably a sort of beginners archaeology, with Dr. Edgar Lee Hewett, Dean of the Summer School—a nothing thing, of which I remember only that one very hot summer day in 1915, when I sat in a stuffy room trying to keep awake and keep studying, the Doctor himself came in with a mixture of pomposity and condescension, straightened a picture on the wall, and, adapting himself to my limited female intellect, told me to remember that museum work was not very different from housework. (I loathed housework and experienced instant disenchantment.) Also, I took intermediate Spanish, which I remember faintly, from some woman with whom I was mutually incompatible. But the only subject that I really remember was linguistics, taught by John Peabody Harrington.

When he walked into the rather dim classroom on that first morning of the summer session, my heart, already strained past endurance, seemed about to stop. I silently and romantically exclaimed that he looked

"like an angry god." I had not hoped so soon to encounter one of those mythical creatures, a scholar, a
scientist, who was also young and beautiful. He *was*
young, although eleven years older than I. I would be
twenty in a month and he had turned thirty-one. He
was tall and thin, with an abrupt, awkward way of
moving. But it was his magnificent head and face that
stirred my imagination. He had dark hair and deep
blue eyes. His splendid forehead was wrinkled into a
scowl and his rather beautiful mouth twisted petulantly.
The simple fact was that he hated teaching, particularly he hated having been inveigled or coerced into
teaching in this summer school, for very little money
and at the sacrifice of time that he might have spent
coaxing half-forgotten words from an ancient informant, someone who might well die even as he wasted
time on this inane collection of normal school aspirants
and silly women who wanted something to fill their
empty days and emptier minds. Even then he was in
the grip of his grand obsession, his compulsion to record all that could be recovered of the remnants of
the cultures, and most especially of the languages, of
the Indians of Southern California. Only here and
there a single old man or old woman, wornout, dis-
couraged, bewildered, clinging precariously to life, survived as the last repository of the speech and lore of
what had been, before the days of the Spanish missions, a flourishing tribe. Universities, rich in en-
dowments, sent expeditions to far-off places. Those
ethnologists who worked intermittently in the California
field were more interested in overall surveys than in
compiling painstaking, detailed records. It must have
seemed to this off-beat, obscure young genius that he
alone perceived the value and the transience of material that might yet be obtained.

All this I would soon learn. What I would be much
slower finding out was that he was as painfully self-
conscious and as unsure of himself as I. He needed
a wise, firm and sympathetic guide, not a youthful
slave and disciple. By the time I realized this, it was

too late; I was no longer interested in the salvage of the man, only in the dissolution of our relationship. Now that he is ten years dead and I am old, I begin to understand that in my place a different sort of woman might—just possibly might—have helped him to fulfill himself both as a scientist and as a human being.

Rebelliously, Harrington came to class wearing a blue shirt, what we then called a "work shirt"—and this at a time when respectable business or professional men wore white shirts as a mark of caste. I was to discover later that underneath the shabby coat most of his shirts were split down the back. That morning, if I noticed at all, it was uncritically. The blue of his shirt emphasized the blue of his eyes.

To him I was in the beginning merely a blob among other blobs. After a few days he began to notice my alertness, to feel, against his will, a response to my eagerness to learn and an even more reluctant emotional response. After several days of drill in phonics, he assigned to his class the task of carefully reading aloud a selection in English of each one's own choosing and transcribing it in phonetic symbols. That would be our first test. It happened that one of my library books on evolution was prefaced by a rather long and—to me at that time—very beautiful poem. I don't remember the author and recall nothing of the poem itself except, "And Thou, O Sea, great mother of my soul," and part of another line, "In me . . . thy billows roll." With great pains, enunciating each word to myself many times, I wrote out the whole poem phonetically. When Harrington returned the graded papers (mostly D's and F's, with a sprinkling of C's), he kept mine and asked me to see him later that afternoon.

In great trepidation I came up to his desk in the empty classroom. He had my exercise before him, and he was touched almost to tears. He said that it was perfect, except for one small mistake—I had written "with" using the symbol for an unvoiced *th* when it should have been voiced. He then asked me to pronounce the word carefully and saw that I had followed accurately my own error of pronunciation. So I had actually turned in a perfect paper! He confided that the subject I had chosen pleased him immeasurably. He, too, was enthralled by the mystique of evolution (although I don't think he ever learned or cared to learn anything of genetics), and it was his great desire to write poetry. We talked a long time. Then we walked together across Cabrillo bridge into the summer sunset——and it would have been beautifully romantic, except that he took such long, rapid strides that I could scarcely keep up with him. We walked through the edge of the Park to Sixth Street, then on to Fifth, where the streetcars ran. There I took a number eleven out towards the pleasant house on Cliff Street that my father had recently bought, and Harrington went the other way, downtown to his shabby workingman's hotel.

There followed for both of us a time of uncertainty and confusion. It was now understood that I should stay after school each afternoon for talk and further instruction, and almost every evening, later and later, we walked across the bridge together. But while he often spoke as if it were completely settled that he and I should spend our lives working together, at other times all his planning left me out completely. Later he explained his reason for blowing hot and cold. He had been, he said, in terrible distress because of his conviction that I must be Jewish. How else could one account for the shape of my nose, and my dark eyes, and my quick intelligence? Of course it wouldn't do to think seriously of marrying a Jew. But then he reminded himself of the Armenians. They were good people, and they weren't so very different from Jews, so perhaps I was an exceptional Jew and it would be possible to marry me. It seemed never to have occurred to him that he might simply have asked me about my racial background. I would have told him that our family was English, Scotch, and Irish, but mostly

Welsh, that my nose was known as "the Chaddock nose" because it had been a feature of my maternal grandfather, a man from New York state and the only Yankee grandparent (and I have since come to suspect very likely of Iroquois origin though my parents would have died rather than admit the possibility of Indian forebears). My dark brown eyes (long since faded to hazel) were not large and liquid like those belonging to the daughters of the Levant; they were small, hooded by heavy upper lids which as I grew older would develop a distinct fold. (This was "the Tucker eyelid," from my father's side of the family, and may also have been an inheritance from some unrecorded mating along the wilderness trail that led from Revolutionary times to the twentieth century, from Virginia to Kentucky, and ultimately to Texas.)

Harrington thought of himself as a native Californian, but this did not imply Spanish ancestry. His parents, who had come west soon after he was born, were old and respectable New England stock. Very old, very respectable—his mother had been born a Peabody. They now lived with the younger son, Robert, and his family on a ranch in the Simi Valley where eggs and walnuts were the principal crops. Harrington had grown up in rural California, in an atmosphere that was frugal and not notably intellectual, though I seem to remember that his mother taught school before her marriage. He had acquired an education by his own efforts, eking out scholarships with hard work. After graduating from Stanford, he had earned money for a year's study in Germany, I think in Leipzig. Naturally, he had traveled steerage, second class would have been a waste of money. Never when we talked about his experience did he say anything that conveyed even faintly the feel of a foreign city, its sights and sounds and smells. But he did tell me at great length how he and a fellow student, a German by birth, had walked the streets of Munich commenting upon new houses; not, he said, that they cared at all whether the houses were new or old, but that each one was listening to the other to see if he would say "noo" or "nyu."

I noticed that most of the teachers in the summer school and virtually all of the colleagues whom Harrington mentioned were addressed as "Doctor." But Harrington said he would never have that title. He never wanted a doctorate because it would involve lectures and offers of teaching positions, and social contacts which he considered artificial and wasteful. This made me a little sad. I still looked wistfully towards the doors of Academe which were now closed to me, because I didn't require a formal education to become this man's helper. I only needed the training he could give me.

Ultimately, when it could be no longer delayed, Harrington came home with me to meet my family. If he had had any lingering doubts about my ethnic suitability, they must have been allayed by my parents, who were unmistakably White and Protestant, Southern-style. He was not at all disturbed to learn that I had an infant daughter. I told him that I was widowed, and he asked no questions. He wasn't, I think, even curious about my personal history. And to him children were scarcely people. He talked later at length about the possibility of bringing up a child without ever talking to it or allowing it to hear human speech in order to see what sort of language it would evolve. In fun, I went along with the fantasy, only to discover that to him it was not fantasy, and that only its impracticality deterred him from undertaking such a project.

At their first meeting, Harrington asked my mother if she didn't think Indians interesting. She hesitated, sniffed and replied, "Interesting maybe; but dirty." Soon afterwards, however, we all went again to visit the Indian Village in Balboa Park, and I at least looked at the people with freshly opened eyes and would have liked to employ an informant on the spot.

Like me, my mother was inclined to be a little in awe of a man with Harrington's educational background, but she was rather appalled by his manners. She had never known a man who thrust himself through a door before the woman who accompanied him, using elbows if necessary. Although our household was far from formal, she also found his table manners not above criticism. I am sure that at the first meal in my parents' home he did not eat his food by his preferred method. This was to cut up everything at once and shovel it in by the tablespoonful, a procedure which saved time, was not "artificial," and promptly produced "that full feeling" which was to him the most pleasurable part of dining. Still he doubtless did talk with his mouth full and gesture with knife in hand. I explained that a man of such genius could not waste time and thought on social niceties. My mother also said that someone really ought to speak to him about his clothes, which were too shabby for "a man in his position." Again I sprang to the defense. He had explained to me, I said, that there was this certain sum of money unjustly withheld from him, and he had taken a sort of vow not to buy anything new until it was paid.

I have long since forgotten who owed him the money and for what. It was bound up in some way with his resentment towards Hewett, but I don't recall what (if any) the connection was. In February of 1915, he had received an appointment as ethnologist on the staff of the Bureau of American Ethnology in the Smithsonian Institution. Quite possibly he was already receiving a salary from that institution and was supposed to be doing fieldwork instead of teaching—but this is mere conjecture from a remote point in time. Eventually the expected sum, or part of it, was finally paid, and Harrington asked me to go with him to pick out new clothes. We went to a cutrate loft and selected, with great care, a very inexpensive suit. It was new and the shirts to wear with it were new. I was enraptured, both at his improved appearance and at the intimacy implied by my having been invited to help. But then I asked him to go to a shoe store with me; he blushed and said he would wait outside. In years to come I wished very much that he had maintained that attitude, and told him so on occasion. After we were married, he felt it his duty to supervise all my expenditures.

Harrington never "took me out" in the conventional sense. All our outings were purposeful, associated in one way or another with linguistics or ethnology. After he had been informed that I had a strain of Welsh blood, he thought it appropriate to take me, one Sunday afternoon, to the meeting of a society where only Welsh was spoken. He briefed me in advance what to listen for, discoursing at length on Welsh phonics and especially the Welsh *l*, a sound occurring in many Indian languages. He would have liked me to learn Welsh, if there had been time.

On another occasion my mother and I went together to hear him lecture for the Theosophical Society at the Temple of Isis, a narrow little hall in downtown San Diego. The theosophists' headquarters and colony of disciples were on Point Loma, where Madame Katherine Tingley reigned supreme. I was fascinated by theosophy in a skeptical sort of way, and I think my mother secretly shared the attraction I felt for teachings that deviated from Protestant Christianity —she had an enquiring mind, held in check by an ingrained concern for her immortal soul. At any rate, we had not infrequently attended lectures at the Temple of Isis. Harrington's subject had something to do with the religious beliefs of American Indians. After the announcements were read, including the customary disclaimer of any connection between Madame Tingley's branch of theosophy and that led by Madame Blavatsky, Harrington was introduced and stepped to the podium. His subject matter was interesting, but poorly presented, and he ducked his head over his notes and mumbled. Because of her partial deafness, my mother heard very little that he said. When he finished, there was a polite but unenthusiastic splatter of applause. Harrington was dismayed because he thought he had failed to "make a good impression"— I believe that was the first time I noticed his use of this phrase, so often on his lips. He did not like to lecture, yet he was far from indifferent to what his audience had thought. I reassured him, then and afterwards, repeating that it had been a very interesting lecture; if, I ventured to add, he had just looked at his audience a little more frequently and spoken a little more clearly, everyone would have appreciated it. Yes, he agreed, he knew he ought to stand straighter. But that wasn't what bothered him. He had said the Mohave believed that after the souls of their departed had wandered for a time they entered into rats or some other small animals before finally ceasing to be.

"I shouldn't have mentioned rats," he lamented. "Those people believe in reincarnation. It was bound to offend them."

"Why? You weren't criticizing their beliefs. You were just talking about the Mohave. It was interesting."

He disagreed. "They took offense. That's why I failed to make a good impression."

"What do you care?" I argued, "you'll never see any of them again." My tone was entirely too light. He looked at me coldly. It was a long time before I realized how traumatic it was for him to suspect that there were those who were unfavorably impressed by his personality.

The lecture must have been given near to the close of summer school. Long before this, our relationship had become very close, although the love affair was not yet consummated. We often walked on the San Diego Exposition grounds, where there were faint trails or no trails at all penetrating the lush shrubbery. One sunny afternoon we scrambled into a hidden bower under a clump of acacia trees. The fragrant, powdery, yellow blossoms fell over us in a pale golden shower. I think it was there he showed me his Phi Beta Kappa key. He was more than proud of it; he regarded it with reverence—which was strange, considering how lightly he professed to hold academic degrees. We talked about it, then we kissed, and he held me in his arms. A park policeman came by and ordered us out gruffly; then recognizing Harrington as one of the instructors, worded his request more politely. He thought we were making love or about to, but we were talking linguistics. Now I was frightfully embarrassed, but Harrington, curiously euphoric, seemed scarcely to hear him. I believe it was the first time he had ever felt pleasure from a woman's physical proximity. We did not leave till the policeman came by a second time.

Shortly after this we had our first real quarrel, not a withdrawal or temporary coolness, but an actual exchange of words. I no longer bought my lunch at one of the pleasant little eating places in the Park. We now ate sandwiches from a paper bag so that Harrington could tutor me in Russian during the lunch hour. He had obtained one of those wretchedly printed blue-backed textbooks from which one learned foreign languages early in the twentieth century (I had owned one like it in Mexico, and had tried to use it to improve my Spanish). It was a very hot day, and we were sequestered in some little cubby of an upstairs room that happened to be unoccupied. I felt languid, sleepy, physically aroused, mentally dull. I had earnestly studied my assignment, but at the moment it all went from me. Harrington was bitterly disappointed in me, and let me know it, harshly. I was supposed to be learning Russian because he had a daydream about our joining an expedition to Siberia. He didn't speak the language himself (although he was, of course, familiar with the phonics and the alphabet), but he thought it would be helpful if I became proficient. That, had I but known it, was a straw in the wind. How many things I would be encouraged or commanded to do because he didn't want to take time from the more important phases of his work! I would type, I would act as chauffeur, I would make contacts that he wished personally to avoid; in short, I would steel myself to do anything and everything that he found boring, frightening, embarrassing, or time-consuming. Ultimately, when I had proven my ability,

I would be sent to do field work on my own, thus substantially increasing his available material. Of these things I had no foresight, no premonition, at the time of the failed Russian lesson. I merely felt hurt at being unfairly treated, and above all I was desolate, because I suspected that he did not love me and my dream was disintegrating. But his irritation passed, and he forgave me when I redeemed myself with better work. (I never did learn Russian. When the fantasy of a Siberian trip failed, I promptly forgot even the Russian alphabet; only to learn it again years later, and again forget it.)

On the whole our relationship suffered few setbacks. My parents considered me desperately self-willed, but I so romanticized my feeling for this man and his way of life that I tried to please him in all things and to make excuses for him whenever he fell short of my ideal. After the summer session was over, I still met him every day for instruction and to help him in his work. I believe we were engaged in putting some of his fieldnotes in order, though I cannot for the life of me recall a single detail. We spent a great deal of time talking—mostly he talked and I listened. He deplored wasting time and tortured himself continually about not accomplishing more, yet I have never known a more proficient time-waster. This seems to be characteristic of persons who drive themselves without respite and eschew all forms of recreation. Harrington had to have work spread out before him; but once it lay there he would launch into long, involved and sometimes pointless discourses, or lose himself in nitpicking trivialities, or stride up and down, running his fingers through his hair and ejaculating, "Procrastination! Procrastination!"

Once towards the end of this period there was a legitimate reason for taking time off. Somewhere in downtown San Diego there was a Philippine exhibit that included a group of Igorotes. These we had to see. I remember the dim light, the shoddy, carnival atmosphere, and the tiny dark people, pathetic as caged

animals. Harrington wanted me to listen carefully to
their speech and to observe their "primitiveness." He
held my arm and told me many things about Igorotes.
Some of their artifacts were on sale and he bought
me a little woven ring. The fact that his first gift to
me was a *ring* seemed marvelously significant. It never
occurred to me that it might have been selected because it was the cheapest object available, and perhaps
it is unfair to think so now; perhaps for him too it
had a symbolic value. At the moment, I was convinced
that he would soon replace it with a "real" ring. He
had confided to me that he had ten thousand dollars,
"all saved when I was working for a very low salary,"
and he had said that he loved me. Surely he would
soon buy me an engagement ring. I was still blissfully
unaware of his detestation of all gems as "artificial"
and extravagant.

That summer and early autumn must have included
a normal amount of fog, including the "high fog"
characteristic of Southern California. I remember only
sunlight and starlight. The marvelously designed Spanish style buildings, built for the San Diego Exposition,
were new then, and the temporary lath-and-plaster
ones looked as solid (almost) as the permanent
California Quadrangle. The effect was that of an
idealized and sanitized version of Spain or Mexico,
the Mexico I knew so well from visits in my childhood, but without its characteristic sounds and smells.
The main avenue was paved, but not with cobblestones,
and from it led no narrow alleyways, ankle-deep in
dust. The arcades cast their heavy shadows, but no
men in soiled white cotton clothes with large hats
lounged in doorways. No laden burros were urged
along, no women swathed in blue *rebozos* bore *ollas*
or trays or bundles on their heads. The odor of stale
pulque did not mingle with the scent of flowers.
Through the crowds of tourists no highborn person-
ages strolled, followed at a respectful three paces by
mozo or *criada,* and no voices clamored or murmured
in Spanish. Still it was all very lovely and picturesque,

even if definitely north of the border. Back and forth, from one end of the park to the other, I trotted at Harrington's heels like a plump, shortlegged puppy. Even when I walked alone I tried to emulate his purposeful stride, and must have made quite a spectacle. A classmate commented, laughing a little unkindly, "I saw you down by the Science of Man building. You were really legging it." By a severe look I attempted to convey the idea that time was not to be wasted.

Then it was early October and everything was changing. Harrington had his office on the second floor of the California building. When we worked late into the night, the janitor, who said he was "as Irish as a barrel of pork packed in Dublin," frequently dropped in and chatted. Harrington encouraged his presence, joked with him, listened intently to his dialect—and afterwards complained of the time that had been consumed. He was increasingly restless, increasingly irritable. One night after the janitor had left, we went out onto the flat roof and sat with our backs against the wall. Bougainvillea mumbled over the parapet and—most wonderfully—a great white owl flew overhead. It should have been an enchanted time, but it was merely sad. Harrington was definitely leaving for the Southwest Museum to collect the notes he had left there and plan his next trip; and, no, it would not be feasible for me to go with him. But I was to learn typing, for that was how I could best prepare myself to help him. There was no break, neither was there any fixed plan for our reunion.

He left. I practiced assiduously on a secondhand Underwood, using a book for self-instruction in touch typing. From him there was a card or two, then nothing. I continued to practice. The plan had been for me to learn to type fast enough to take Harrington's dictation. With this in mind, my mother was pressed into service to read aloud to me. She soon "drew the line" and also "put her foot down" on reading from heavy works on anthropology, but said she would continue to cooperate if allowed to substitute stories from various magazines. Halfway through December I had typed any number of stories from the *Cosmopolitan* and *The Ladies' Home Journal,* and *McClure's* and what have you, and had become fairly proficient, but my heart was a lump of grief and disappointment. I stopped wearing "my ring." Although I tried to interest myself in preparations for my child's Christmas, to act bright and natural, I never had a poker face and went around wretched. Mother sympathized with me and shielded me from my father's remarks. They both thought Harrington had "trifled with my affections," just as, throughout their association with him, they tried persistently to interpret his actions in terms of ordinary human vices and virtues. Even then I knew better. More likely he had become absorbed in some project and forgotten me, or had decided that I would be more hindrance than help.

A few days before Christmas, at dusk, a messenger came to the door with a parcel. From him to me. It was a suitcase, the second gift and the last that I remember receiving. My mother thought that it was a very odd present for a man to give to a young woman; but we agreed that it was significant—that he must intend for me to join him.

That winter of 1915-1916 the rains came. They came relentlessly. Dams washed out. We and our neighbors stood on the bluff back of our house that overlooked the normally dry San Diego River and watched dead animals, parts of buildings, and other debris borne on a raging torrent out to sea. Rail service to Los Angeles was interrupted and travel between the two cities had to be by boat. This seemed to me an adequate reason for not receiving any communication in regard to the suitcase. I knew from the return address on it that Harrington was still to be reached at the Southwest Museum in Los Angeles, and I could wait no longer to know where I stood with him. Besides I wanted the adventure of a boat trip.

I shared a cabin with a mother and daughter, both very fat, who conversed endlessly about food and deplored the lack of music in the dining salon. They could, it seems, dine much more pleasurably to music. I had never eaten to music, so was unable to offer an opinion. When we disembarked, a taxi driver directed me to a small, old and respectable hotel, the Angelus. Timid about going down alone to the dining room, I ordered dinner in my room—tomato soup and fresh salmon steak. That was the last touch of innocent luxury I was to enjoy for some time to come.

In the morning I got in touch with Harrington, and he came to me promptly, looking like a thunder-cloud. Didn't I know, he asked, wasn't I aware that there were places where I could stay *a whole week* for less than the three dollars per day that I was paying? He ordered me to pack at once, took my bag, set it down to ask for my bill, and snatched it back quickly from the alert bellhop. Harrington did not, under any circumstances, approve of giving tips; while I, unfortunately, have all my life enjoyed tipping generously.

Walking along the street at our usual breathtaking pace, his temper cleared. He even walked beside me, rather than a step or two ahead. It became obvious that he was very glad indeed to see me, that all the old attraction was there, and that by my unannounced arrival I had delivered him from the horns of some secret dilemma. He installed me in a fleabag hotel on what was even then skid row, and that evening we dined at a restaurant run by a Chinese (but not serving Chinese food), where one could get plenty to eat for a quarter. We talked late that night. After Harrington left, I was afraid and propped a chair against my door. However, after I had stayed there two or three days without being molested, I became resigned if not accustomed to my surroundings and was not afraid anymore. Harrington spent a great deal of time with me, talking, talking, pouring out his longings, frustrations, and plans. When I took the boat back to San Diego, it was definitely arranged that he would send for me shortly. This time I had no doubts.

II First Field Trips In Rural California

FROM THIS POINT until that parting which marked the beginning of the end of our association, my memories are very seldom in chronological order. Here and there something can be dated; but I have no letters, no documents of any kind, remaining from this period of my life. There is merely a jumble of impressions, of vignettes bright or lurid, a few of which happen to correspond with remembered dates, private or historical. I cannot always say, for example, which episodes belong to our first stay in Santa Ynez in 1916 and

17

which to subsequent visits; I do not know when we drove through the mud and driving rain to Coalinga or when we stayed with or near a group of Indians camped by the tule swamp near Lemoore, and I sat on the cold, damp ground all night long watching the medicine man dance, except that both occasions must have been in the winter. Nor do I know when we visited that remote ranchería near the headwaters of the Tule River, except that it was mid or late summer, and not our first year together. Over all there is the glamor of youth and adventure, the bitter fog of disappointment, and the deceptive veil of a persistent illusion.

I do remember arriving in Santa Ynez in the spring of 1916, though I don't recall whether I got there by bus or horse-drawn stage. I have not forgotten the green beauty of the countryside or the thrill when Harrington met me and I knew that I was to share his life and his career. I remember also my own foolish vanity and optimism. I carried the suitcase he had sent me and wore a navy blue skirt with white shirtwaist, and a navy blue straw hat with a red feather. I was resolved that, no matter what wilds we traveled in, I would always keep myself neat and attractive. So much for resolutions. The hat was soon lost, the blouse worn out, but the skirt lasted on; first spotted, then really soiled, then dirt-encrusted till it would all but stand alone. That dreadful blue serge skirt conditioned me, so that to this day if I am consulted about the color of a dress, I say, "Anything but navy blue." But at the time, at the beginning, having always had decent clothes I assumed that I always would.

Harrington's informant in Santa Ynez was a very ancient Chumash woman, María Solares. She must have been ninety or thereabouts. Her gentle face had the softness and fragility of something very old. Harrington took me to visit her and had me listen to her Chumash words, while he smiled and cupped his ear and asked her to repeat until her patience wore thin. Sometimes he would ask me about the way a word had sounded to me, but I was not yet trusted to record anything on my own.

María spoke no English, and it pleased Harrington that I had enough Spanish to make myself understood. She asked him, during an interview at which I was not present, if I was *católica*. Remembering that I had once mentioned receiving infant baptism in the Methodist church, he told her I was *metodista,* and that it was really the same thing. She enquired then if they *"ponen la cruz arriba"* (put the cross above, presumably on top of the churches), and being assured that they did, she relaxed and said I would be a proper wife for him. I have no idea what María thought Harrington's religion was; he scarcely knew enough ritual to deceive her. Perhaps she thought religion was more important for a woman than a man. Certainly she felt fondness and therefore a certain responsibility for him; invariably courteous, she frequently treated him with the indulgence that one would accord a child or a harmless madman.

I typed information which could be typed, and copied by hand Chumash words containing sounds for which there were no symbols on the Underwood. All this was put onto "slips," not cards but pieces of paper cut to the size that Harrington had decided was most convenient and printed with lines according to his specifications. (In matters connected with his work, he was not averse to spending money, though he always wanted to get good value.) Those slips were filed (at the time) in cardboard boxes, a duplicate having been made for each Indian word and miscellaneous item of information, so that they could be cross-filed. Material piled up rapidly, and at one time got so far ahead of us that Harrington hired a local high school girl, and I undertook to teach her our system of filing. The experiment did not work out, but I remember that he spoke admiringly of my patience and skill as a teacher. He really smiled at me then, not a "hope to make a good impression" smile, but a genuine and natural, warm and even loving smile, and I bloomed in its light.

Now I cannot, for the life of me, remember a single word of María's native tongue, but other things that she said I shall never forget.

She had been told that before cattle were brought in to graze the land, the wild oats and other grasses had grown waist-high or even shoulder-high, and among the grass the lupine and other wildflowers all grew lush and tall, not stunted as we see them now. In those days the hunters did not have to go afield, for deer and elk fed right outside the doors of the houses of the People. That had been in the good years. But once there came a great drought, the game went away, and there were no acorns, no seeds to gather, no roots to dig. This went on for several years. Many died. Women put hot water on their breasts to try to make milk to give their men strength, and all the fragments of buckskin, even the moccasins, were boiled and chewed. When finally all had resigned themselves to death, a runner came over the mountains from the village located near the site of what is now the town of Gaviota. He cried out that a whale was stranded on the beach. The people streamed through the rugged mountain passes and down to the sea, carrying those who were too feeble to walk. There they feasted and grew strong. The decaying whale was big enough to nourish many people for a long time. When it was all gone, the rains came again, and the grasses and the game.

María also had stories and legends of mission and post-mission times. Her grandmother, she said, had been *esclava de la misión*. She had run away many, many times, and had been recaptured and whipped till her buttocks crawled with maggots. Yet she had survived to hand down her memories of the golden age before the white men came. Now her descendants were all very good Catholics.

A narrative of much more recent date concerned the dreadful fate that had almost befallen an Indian girl who was very beautiful and wild. She had an insatiable appetite for men, and it was implied that she might even have cast her eyes upon a young priest. Returning late one moonless night to her grandmother's home, she knew that something pursued her. She rushed into the house, slammed the door and pulled in the latch string. But there was still the cat hole, that little hole cut at the base of the door where the cat could go in and out at will. The long black arm of the Devil snaked through it and stretched clear across the room, extending a great hairy clawed hand toward that unfortunate and undeserving girl. Had it not been that her grandmother was armed with something sacred—what I do not recall; it may have been a fragment of a palm branch left over from Palm Sunday or a blessed candle or even a little vial of holy water—she would surely have come to a most dreadful end. But threatened with the power of the Church, the monstrous arm of Satan shriveled and retreated.

These were the tales which lent their own peculiar patina to the places where I wandered. Actually, I cannot have had much time for wandering alone, but in retrospect these wanderings loom very large. The whole land was so exquisitely beautiful, so new to me and yet so mournfully touched with the light of its irretrievable past, María's lost Eden, in which fantasy and unwritten history were inextricably mingled. The roads were narrow and dusty, bordered by wild rose and elderberry bushes in full bloom. The stream was swift, clear, and shallow, winding sometimes through trees that met above it. In such a place, I saw a salmon, caught it with my hands, then put it back, not realizing that it had already completed its life cycle. At another time I watched a small, smooth, red, large-eyed creature walking slowly with primeval awkwardness over the smooth stones at the water's edge. I truly thought it was something not of this world, or at least hitherto unknown to men. Even after Harrington said it was a newt and not at all uncommon, the enchantment lingered.

Once, just once, during our first summer in Santa

Ynez, Harrington took the whole day off from work. We walked away from the town, roaming over honey-colored hills dotted with great oak trees, their foliage so dark that it was almost black. Here and there grew clumps and thickets of lesser trees and shrubs, all strange to me because all of rural California was new and strange. Harrington knew their names, popular and scientific, but I remember only the buck-eye with its creamy blossoms. It was an idyllic day. As we spoke of the Indians who had gathered acorns for centuries on these very hillsides, Harrington had an inspiration. He thought it would be beautiful and ap-propriate that we should take our clothes off and go about in a state of nature. The outcome was not happy. By nightfall I was suffering a high fever from sunburn.

From the beginning much of our life together was far from idyllic. Harrington found me resentful and even quarrelsome over matters that seemed to him un-important or entirely reasonable. When María and her relatives visited us in the house we had rented, I was expected to provide large and heavy meals. Not know-ing anything about cooking and being in the first stages of pregnancy, at a period when the smell of food kept overnight without refrigeration and, in fact, almost all food made me queasy, I protested. But I soon learned that it would always be my duty to cook for inform-ants and resigned myself to it. Then Harrington stirred up discord again by supervising my task in the interest of curbing waste. In those days one could buy squares of concentrated *chili con carne* which, cut up and boiled, made a rich, hot greasy dish. Occasionally, we would get hold of some that had been kept too long and was honey-combed with flecks of mold, but for the most part it was fresh and appetizing. Sometimes when I had just one square of chile to provide for several people with hearty appetites, I would supplement it by breaking eggs into it and poaching them in the sauce. One day I did this while Harrington was watching. He picked up a discarded eggshell and pointed out the small amount of egg white adhering to it. Then he delivered a lecture on my deliberate waste of nutritious food. He said that I could scrape out each shell carefully with a teaspoon. I retorted that eggs cooked quickly and had to be handled quickly, and that there was no time to scrape each shell. It wouldn't take but a few seconds, he replied, and this, he was sure, was what his mother would have done—although he had to admit that he had never actually watched her doing it. Thereafter, I tried to cook eggs when his attention was engaged elsewhere.

Once in the heat of summer we literally came to blows. The argument may have been over the sheets —though how there happened to be sheets on the bed at all, I'm sure I don't know. We had only one pair, and after weeks of use they were gray with soil and flecked with minute specks of blood from the bites of ubiquitous sand fleas. I returned to a continuing argument that the time was long past to buy another pair and send these sheets out to be washed—of course, I ultimately ended up washing them myself in a galvanized bucket too small for the job. Anyway whether or not this was the pretext, we quarrelled violently, and I struck the first blow, as much in frustration as in anger, and subconsciously perhaps to see how he would react. He struck back, feebly and ineptly. If he had simply looked at me, if he had held my arms and restrained me, even if he had knocked me down, my respect for him would not have been lessened. As it was, for just a moment before shame and remorse overcame me, I experienced a curious flash of detachment, freedom, almost exultation. The illusion that I was a loved and loving woman was almost shattered then and there, but I clung to it, held it together by force of will.

Soon after we were married, Harrington decided we should have a car. It would greatly enhance our mobility, and we could visit otherwise inaccessible places in the company of aged or infirm informants. He sent to Los Angeles for literature on the various makes, and we soon narrowed our choice to two, a Ford or a

Dodge (I think—if they were manufacturing Dodges in 1916). I thought we might go to Los Angeles together and look them over, but he said there was no point at all in both of us going. After all, I was the one who would do the driving. Since that was the case, I thought I should have the right of choice. I preferred the non-Ford, and for a time Harrington agreed. Then, the night before I was to leave to pick up the car, he decided that we should thrash it out all over again. He finally settled on the Ford, which was, undoubtedly, the right decision since only a Model T could have stood up under the abuse to which that car would be subjected. I agreed because there was no use in disagreeing, and said that, in view of the fact that tomorrow would be a long day, I should like to get some rest. But Harrington felt that he must marshall his arguments, over and over. This went on all night long. I tried not answering, but he went on talking. I wept with fatigue, but Harrington said that such an important matter should be thoroughly considered. In the morning I took the bus (or was it a combination of bus and train?) to Los Angeles, trembling with nerves, fatigue, and a merciless headache.

There must indeed be a Providence that watches over fools and the foolhardy. By noon I had bought the car, paying in cash—even then, even before World War I, when he developed a fear that the banks might close, Harrington usually carried a considerable sum of money on his person, and he had given me the purchase price plus a little extra for expenses. The salesman handed me the necessary papers and explained the operation of the vehicle. This pedal was the clutch, that one the brake, and the reverse was in the middle. This lever was the emergency brake, which you must always set before cranking the car. These two levers on the steering wheel were the spark and the throttle. Retard your spark and then advance it after the motor caught. He explained to me about right and left turns, sat beside me while I drove around the block a couple of times, said I caught on quick, and sent me on my way.

I got lost in Carpenteria. It wasn't a very big town, but I couldn't find the right way out. I ran two wheels up over a sidewalk and was embarrassed. At a service station I "filled her up" and got directions. It was dark when I headed up Gaviota Pass, thinking for a moment of the runner who had gone that way to carry news of the stranded whales numbly hoping that as he made it on foot I might make it in this car. The yellow lights, dimming or brightening as the four-cylinder engine labored or speeded up, cast their uncertain illumination on the winding road. I felt that I would probably drive off over a cliff. At best, the car would stall, and I wouldn't be able to start it. Finally there was nothing left but car and night and endless, endless road. I was beyond fatigue, beyond pain, beyond fear.

After eleven o'clock I stopped in front of our little frame house and staggered inside on shaking legs. Harrington was pleased that I had brought the car back without mishap.

In the morning we went out to inspect our purchase and found a flat tire—how long it had been flat, God only knows! Harrington helped with the jack, then went back to his work. I sat in the dust trying to pry the tire off the rim. Finally someone stopped by and helped me, but not before I had cut the tube beyond repair by injudicious efforts with the tire iron. Afterwards Harrington learned to change tires, unwillingly acknowledging that it was a task I wasn't adapted to perform.

After my baptism of fire, I found I loved to drive. And I grew over-confident. Going along a narrow road a little faster than was advisable, the right wheel entered a patch of heavy sand, and I couldn't turn it back again. The car went its own course over a bank, falling with what seemed great deliberation on its side on top of a stand of young eucalyptus trees, which let us down rather gently. No one was hurt. Harrington had been in the back seat with an Indian to whom we were giving a lift, and they both scrambled out and I heard him calling, "Are you all right? Are you all right?" This was a memory I cherished for a long time. It had been a genuine, spontaneous expression of concern for my welfare.

I was all right except for bruises and a rather painful spot in my right side. The Indian walked away disgusted. Harrington went up to a nearby farmhouse. The people were Danish, very hospitable. They saw to having the car hauled away, and invited us to stay with them while repairs were being made by the nearest garageman in collaboration with a blacksmith. Our accident had happened in the Danish community of Solvang, a settlement of Old Country farmers which was still many years away from spawning a tourist trap baited with smorgasbord and Danish pastry. We stayed at that farm several days. The hurt in my side gradually got better, but I was grateful for the rest and enjoyed the cleanliness and good food. Harrington was delighted with the opportunity it gave me to hear Danish spoken. He told me to listen particularly for the glottal stop. Danish was full of it, as were many Indian languages.

When we got our car back, I was not nervous about driving, although I had learned a lesson about roads with "soft shoulders." Harrington was nervous. Although another car had not been involved, he flinched and cringed at approaching traffic, estimated the distance in inches between meeting or passing cars, and told me repeatedly it was only my ignorance of physics which kept me from realizing the terrible consequences of collision at thirty miles per hour. This sort of conversation was not calming to the nerves, especially when I was over-tired. I sometimes replied untactfully. I failed to recognize or sympathize with his deep, ingrained fears, and the resultant tensions, which must have been all the more agonizing because of his efforts to repress them.

We went back to Harrington's "headquarters," the

Southwest Museum, and I was presented to the founder and curator, Charles F. Lummis. Lummis was one of those older, superior, established persons whom Harrington regarded with a mixture of fear, envy, and self-protective scorn. I, of course, was in awe of him. I only talked with him briefly once or twice, and vaguely remember that he was brilliant, abrasive, witty and probably himself quite eccentric. Harrington was concerned about the impression I might make. I must at least have aroused the great man's sympathy, for he wrote a letter addressed to me alone. I showed it to Harrington, and then, in anger, destroyed it. It would have been better if I had kept it to myself, pondered its advice, and preserved it as an interesting souvenir. In it, in an acerbic way, Lummis wished me happiness, but doubted if I would attain it unless I was prepared to be a combination of mother, nurse-maid, and business manager and to exercise firm control; on the other hand, he wrote, if I expected to be "uplifted and upborne on the wings of genius" I was in for a bitter disappointment. Unfortunately, I did still expect to be uplifted and upborne on the wings of genius.

Harrington never let Lummis know that he had seen the letter, and he continued to use the facilities of the museum. He had an office there where he worked over his material and kept it safely stored. Since all tasks took longer than the time allotted, we would often go to Los Angeles for two or three days and end up staying two weeks. When we traveled about in remote places or with no settled address, mail was delivered to the Museum and held there till called for.

During our stays in the city, Harrington felt that, since we had the car, a hotel room would be an unnecessary expense. After our day's work, we would drive out of town to a relatively unoccupied area and sleep on the ground beside the car. One night we were aroused by a flashlight shining in our faces. It seemed that the police viewed with suspicion our camping out in that locality. Thereafter, we had to drive further.

I remember waking early in mornings drenched in fog that was milky white and smelled of the sea. Closer to the heart of the city, the traffic was already heavy and exhaust fumes were beginning to pollute the air. Grimy and disheveled, we ate breakfast at "the China-man's," then drove to the museum, where I would wash my face and attempt to put my hair in some sort of order and Harrington would shave. Then followed a long day typing letters and field notes, putting the Indian words on slips and sorting them, learning about language-patterns, and many other things. If Harring-ton's mood was good, all our work was punctuated with talk, some of it fantastic, and daydreaming. Lunch was always stale bread and cheese. Near the restaurant where we ate breakfast and dinner was a Chinese laundry, where Harrington had his shirts and some of my clothes done, so that outwardly we were fairly clean; but I longed for a bath.

Perhaps my most vivid memory connected with the Southwest Museum was of crossing a narrow elevated walkway that led to the rear entrance. A fighting rooster sometimes appeared to dispute my passage—neurotically, I believed that he lay in wait for me—and since I always had my arms full of books and manuscripts, I could not defend myself. This was the only animal that I ever remember fearing in all my life. He usually managed to bloody my shins in two or three places. Harrington thought my reaction rather laughable. "That chicken doesn't bother me at all," he said. "Naturally not," I retorted, "he can't peck through your trousers." However, he *was* afraid of a rather large and vicious-looking dog who sometimes seemed inclined to guard the museum. Once this dog actually grasped my forearm in his jaws. We exchanged a long look, he did not close his teeth, and after that our re-lations were neutral if not precisely friendly.

Harrington disliked the expressions "fieldwork" and "in the field." For some reason they struck him as artificial and pretentious. "Even my mother," he said in the tone of one who has suffered the ultimate betrayal, "talks about my being 'in the field.'"

Of course, these were terms which we had to employ in his letters to Washington, and perhaps it was this association which made them distasteful. He appreciated the fact that only his position with the Bureau of American Ethnology enabled him to do the work that had already become his lifework, and he lived in terror of losing it. But he also had a paranoiac belief that every man's hand was against him, that at any moment he might be forced to go to Washington and remain there, to publish work that he was not ready to publish, and to see his most precious discoveries appropriated by someone else. Therefore all letters and reports must create "a good impression" and at the same time be as devious as possible, revealing very little of his real activities and plans. He wanted them to show tremendous (if vague) achievements, which needed a little more, just a little more time and money to complete. He struggled over these documents and often appealed to me to help him word them. Even his signature was cause for anxiety. I must always put a straight line where he could write it with care, for it would not do to have his name slanted up or down. The preparation of an expense account was no less of an ordeal. It constituted a waste of time and a potential trap. Every penny must be accounted for—later, when I was in Washington, my close friend, Miss May S. Clark, whose duty it was to check over these accounts, told me how she had been impressed by the recurring item: "5 lbs. boiling beef @ 5¢ per lb." When it came to adding up the long columns of figures, Harrington disdained the conventional method. He counted under his breath, very rapidly, touching his pencil twice to four points on the figure eight, once each to three, then two points on the five, four then three points on the seven, etc. I was intrigued and more than a little shocked. I made it a point of honor to say "eight and five are thirteen and seven are twenty," and frequently made mistakes; he counted out loud "like a moron" and made no mistakes. Anything else, he said, was a waste of time.

One of our trips that first summer was to visit an old couple living on a scrap of land near San Luis Obispo. On the way we stopped at Pismo Beach to dig clams, getting thoroughly stuck at dusk on a sandy road leading up from the sea. After some futile efforts to dig out, Harrington decided that we should spread our blankets in front of the car and sleep there till daylight. Long after dark an old man came in a wagon and had to pull his mules around us. We laughed for days at the outraged way he had grumbled to himself, *"En el puro camino"* (in the pure [middle of the] road).

We paid our hosts for information and meals, and ate with them, except for several meals exclusively of clams, which they did not care to share. The husband must have been the principal informant, for Harrington spent most of his time with him. I became well acquainted with the wife, chatting with her in my broken Spanish, while she did her housework and prepared meals. One day she set me to peeling vegetables for a stew while she fetched strips of jerky from where they hung outside the house. The meat was flyspecked and somewhat green in places from the damp coastal air. But I resolved to eat my share. I was beginning to understand that people who lived on the edge of starvation cannot afford to be finicky, and already life with Harrington had cured me of much of my squeamishness. Besides the woman washed all the ingredients for her stew carefully and cooked them a long time.

This woman impressed me as a very cleanly person. I can still see her long, thin, pale brown hands, always scrupulously clean, moving about in a deft and practiced manner. But when I said something about bathing in the sea, she remarked that she had not touched water, salt or fresh, to any part of her body except her hands and face for over forty years. Bathing, she said, could be hazardous to the health. When she was a young girl, she had washed her body constantly, and had been very sickly. Then a doctor had advised her never to bathe again, and taking his advice, she had ever since remained in perfect health What kind of a person, I wondered, had given such advice? I did not understand till long after that the "doctor" had been a shaman, and I do not recall that Harrington clarified the matter for me. At that time, he, too, though far ahead of me, was young in his understanding of the ways of the People.

Come to think of it, I may never have mentioned the matter to him for fear it might reenforce his slovenly habits. In spite of all the evidence before his eyes and nose, Harrington tended to equate "primitiveness" with dirt, with a sort of deliberate wallowing, and to use this as an excuse for his own lack of fastidiousness. This was the attitude that he maintained, though he had been amused at my mother's generalization about Indians. And while he thought that anything primitive was to be admired and emulated, he did not approve of intermarriage with Indians or with any non-Nordic race. If the races intermarried, he said, everybody would look alike, everybody would have a sort of muddy-brown complexion and a mediocre intellect.

The couple at San Luis Obispo had been married for a long time and were always courteous with each other. Harrington and I had been married a short time and frequently quarreled. I determined to come to some understanding with him on the matter of finances. I was already accepting many of his notions of economy. I understood the importance of his work and sympathized with what he felt to be the precariousness of his position—in view of the long years through which his association with the Bureau would endure, it was probably less precarious then he believed, but I had been infected by his sense of insecurity. However, I needed clothing suitable to my advancing pregnancy, and it galled me never to have a penny to spend. Remembering my parents' long conflict about money and the way in which it had been at last resolved I decided to propose a similar solution.

We were sitting on the ground, on the farther side of the car. The air was somewhat tainted with the stench of dead and dying clams, for we had taken more than we could use and the remainder lay in the shade covered by a wet gunnysack—I having already learned that to throw away food or potential food, no matter what its condition, was to provoke an explosion.

Screwing up my courage, and interrupting Harrington's train of thought, I asked, "Could you give me a sort of an allowance, a little money each month, no matter how little, so I could save up for things I need and have something in my purse for emergencies?"

Harrington listened in stunned silence, while I went on to elaborate my proposal, which seemed to me quite reasonable.

He looked at me with loathing, with that familiar furrowed brow and scornfully twisted mouth. "I never heard of anything so degrading," he responded coldly, "it would be like paying you to be my wife."

He stalked off in anger, and I relieved my frustration somewhat by throwing away the clams, since I had heard that stale seafood could be poisonous. He would, if he condescended to speak again that day, criticize my wastefulness, but such criticisms were quite common.

Harrington frequently cooked large pots of mush, cornmeal, or cream of wheat, which he always referred to as *polenta*. This would be his staple article of diet long after, in hot weather, it began to ferment. Sometimes in his absence, I would clean out the pot and wash it, claiming to have eaten the remainder. We had many quarrels over food, but the worst that I remember, not this first year that we were together but the next, was over a can of corn. We were carrying about with us a can which had become battered, possibly punctured, and seemed to be puffed out at the ends. One chilly morning on the Ridge Route south of Bakerfield, after a night spent in the car, he suggested that we should have corn (eaten cold, of course, out of the can) for breakfast, and this damaged can was the only one remaining. When he went away from the car for a few moments, I threw it as hard and as far as I could over a cliff, where he could not possibly retrieve it.

None of these dissensions created a permanent rift, though every evidence of my lack of thrift was disillusioning to Harrington. And although I did not then realize it, every quarrel ripped at the fabric of my affection for him, which was more fragile—or perhaps the word is shoddy—than I believed at the time.

III   A Small Adobe On Tejon Ranch

STARTING OUT FROM Bakersfield, we drove up to the small ranchería hidden within the immense Tejon Ranch. Now for the first time there were Indians all around us. The nearest place where a white family lived and where English was spoken was the ranch store, some ten miles down the road. Here we were away from the coast and coastal influences. These people spoke a Shoshonean language. I don't know why I can't remember a single word of it—possibly because my work was still mainly copying, sorting and filing.

It was an uphill climb all the way from the floor of the San Joaquin Valley to the Tejon Ranch store; then more steeply upgrade, through rolling hills, to the ranchería, beyond which the Coastal Range rose abruptly, so that this whole small community was on a slope. Even the minute fields and vegetable gardens were atilt.

We occupied a one-room adobe just at the edge of the brush and oak-covered slopes. There was one other adobe close by which belonged to a pleasant, attractive, youngish woman named Juana. Below these houses a bare, grassy expanse of land inclined gently and endlessly. A small stream, cold even in summer, angled into and then ran parallel with this downward sloping field. I think it was about a hundred yards from our place to the stream, but then I have never had a good eye for judging distance. Sometimes it seemed very far. We had a large pot, but it was generally full of mush or beans, and besides it was awkward to carry when full of water. I fetched water for the house in a canteen, and sometimes I carried the tin plates and other eating utensils down to the creek and scoured them out with gravel. The road, such as it was, approached our adobe from above, from the back of the house, and that was where the car was parked, its wheels blocked with stones. To reach the house you had to climb through, over, or squirm under a barbed wire fence. There may have been another fence between the house and the stream, but if so, I don't remember it. Juana's was the only house we could see. The other houses in the village, some of wood and some of adobe, were scattered at random and at considerable distance from each other up the wooded slopes.

Our house was furnished with a rough table, two or three crude chairs, and a wood-burning cookstove. Besides the pot and our tin plates and cups, we had a skillet and a tin washbasin. Our light was a kerosene lantern. We spread our quilts and blankets on the dirt floor, which I never learned to keep hardpacked like Juana's. The effete niceties of sheets, clean or dirty, were long since left behind. There were no toilet facilities; one simply went into the brush. This posed less of a sanitation problem than might be assumed. The numerous lean dogs had acquired the habit of eating human excrement, and they took care of all solid waste matter as soon as it was deposited. This disgusted me to the point of nausea. It seemed horribly unnatural. But Harrington explained that man's diet was so unnaturally rich that other animals could properly find nourishment in his waste. He assured me this was the case even with our diet in which I had not noticed any excessive richness. He assured me that we did indeed eat much more food and much richer food than our bodies could assimilate.

Once a week we drove down to the store for supplies and to pick up any mail that might have been forwarded there. On one of these occasions, it must have been about the middle of December, Harrington was excited to find an invitation to attend a meeting of his colleagues at Berkeley. I don't know whether or not he was invited to read a paper, but I remember that he was both flattered and apprehensive. A. L. Kroeber of the University of California, Berkeley, was to preside, or at least to be there, and Kroeber loomed over his professional life like a menacing giant. Harrington envied his status, his resources, the facility and regularity with which he published, and at the same time held his linguistic abilities in something like contempt, believing that his work in this line lacked thoroughness, that his Indian words were poorly heard and carelessly recorded. Besides, nothing could convince him that Kroeber was not a Jew.

For once, there was no period of indecision as to whether to attend. Harrington said that I should drive him down to the store the next morning; then he could catch a ride into Bakersfield, take the train for Los Angeles, pick up his clothes and necessary papers, and just have time to make the convention, seminar or whatever.

I wanted to go and put up a strong argument. I may have been ashamed to say that I was afraid to be left alone, because such fear would not have been consonant with my role of "a woman who thought like a man." The fear was there, but even more compelling was my youthful hunger for change and companionship, for meeting people of the larger world. I argued that I could buy a maternity dress and be presentable. Harrington asked, did I want to be the only woman there? I said the other men must have wives and families, and I could do whatever they did, and at least I could meet these anthropologists and ethnologists of whom I stood in awe. Harrington said I would meet people when we went to Washington, which would be all too soon. Anyway, they were all very boring and not to be trusted, and the whole idea of my going along was extravagant, unsuitable and not to be considered; and he'd only be gone four days at most.

Returning alone to the adobe, I felt very isolated. The miles stretched hugely all around. I was as shy as the people of the ranchería and as yet had exchanged only a few words with one or two of them. They spoke only their own language and Spanish. The first I knew not at all, and in the latter I was far from fluent. I realized that I wouldn't hear a word of English till Harrington returned.

The door of the adobe was held shut by a fragile hook and staple arrangement. Anybody could pull it open. Saturday night some of the men of the village got drunk. It was literally their night to howl. They did not approach my house but I could hear them in the dark and otherwise silent night. Memories of stories I had heard in childhood about Apaches and Comanches arose to haunt me. The men howled and the coyotes answered them. I shivered under my dusty blankets with my hand on the handle of a dull axe. In the morning, I was less fearful, but very glad that Harrington would soon be back. I knew that he always accomplished projects quicker in planning than in actuality and that he might be gone for a week. But at least after four days I could begin to expect him.

Into the second week, I began to worry. I decided to try to start the Ford and drive down to the store. I was running low on food, and although I had very little money I could at least buy something and see if there was a letter. I retarded the spark, set the handbrake, and struggled manfully with the crank. The engine caught, misfired, and died, but the shock was enough to jar loose the insufficiently blocked wheels. The car started to roll slowly. I jumped out of the way, tried to get in and couldn't, and watched helplessly as it bumped its way down the rocky slope and came to rest against a sagging barbed wire fence.

Now I was really alone, really helpless. I think I went a little crazy. Time would go on and on, relentlessly. I would have my baby untended on a dirt floor and die in childbirth. I told myself that Harrington was already dead. I would not believe that any man could bring himself to leave a wife (whom he said he loved) alone in the eighth month of pregnancy, without food, money, or transportation—not yet accepting the fact that this man was cast in a different mold and could easily do such a thing, with no sense of dereliction and without intentional cruelty. Each morning was colder than the last. The fragments of a nursery rhyme kept running through my head, blotting out all rational thought: "The north wind will blow/and we shall have snow/and what will poor robin do then?" Providentially, going down to the creek for water early one frosty morning, I actually saw a robin. He was not poor robin; on the contrary, he was plump, saucy, and self-assured. He brought me a flash of sanity, a fleeting conviction that all would be well.

By this time all that remained of our stock of canned goods was one can of salmon, which I determined to save "till the last," whatever that might be. Meanwhile I lived off flour gruel, with a little very tough bacon rind. Naturally this diet produced constipation.

When I went into the brush, the dogs aggravated my problem. Juana had a great black dog named Oso (Bear), gentle (or as gentle as any of the dogs thereabouts) but monstrous in size. He could place his paws on my shoulders as I stood erect and look almost directly into my eyes. Oso drove the other dogs away, and for this I was grateful; but when he pushed against me as I squatted and knocked me down, I would lie on the hard ground, covered with stones and sharp twigs, and cry helplessly. I liked Oso and was not really afraid of him. I knew my neurotic fancy that he would find it an easy transition from human excrement to human flesh was no more than a sick imagining. But all the same the notion recurred.

One morning Juana had evidently been watching for me to come out. She beckoned me to her and gave me a beautiful, crisp green head of cabbage from her garden. Perhaps it was Christmas morning or very close to it, and the cabbage may have been a Christmas present. I know I have never received a more appreciated gift. Most of it I ate raw, the rest I boiled with bacon rind. It relieved my physical discomfort, and my courage got its second wind. I went farther afield to gather small enough branches to break with the dull axe, and kept up a fire instead of sitting hopelessly in the cold. One day a man from the village, possibly at Juana's instigation, brought my accumulated mail from the ranch store.

There were several letters from Harrington, affectionate and full of enthusiasm. The story they unfolded had nothing to do with the long concluded meeting at the University. It seems that in Los Angeles he had found a man who would make metal boxes exactly to his specifications to hold his precious "slips." These boxes would protect his material from mice and weather, and would greatly facilitate sorting and filing. He had, naturally, stayed to supervise the work, but would return in a few days. Somehow this left me singularly cold. The really important item in the mail was a parcel from my mother, a cardboard box containing a sizable chunk of Christmas fruitcake. It was rich, delicious, filled with nuts and candied fruits, liberally spiked with brandy and superbly nourishing. Her accompanying letter was reproachful. They had expected me home for Christmas, my child had missed me, it had been sometime since they had heard from me. I ate the fruitcake, a little at a time, well-salted with tears, and it is hard to say if I wept for remorse, loneliness, homesickness, self-pity, or sheer gratitude.

After dark one evening, before the fruitcake was entirely consumed, Harrington returned. He had caught a ride on a wagon up from the store. On his shoulder he carried a gunnysack with a few groceries and two of the metal boxes. They were to loom large in my life for the next few years, but I found the food of more immediate interest. It was hard for Harrington to understand this, harder still for him to understand why I had wasted time feeling sad and crying and why I seemed to blame him for something. Neither did he know why I was suddenly insisting on going home immediately. He had suggested, months before, that to have the baby there with an Indian woman to help would be a way to open up invaluable information, both ethnological and linguistic. But I had been absolutely adamant. I would have the child in my parent's house in San Diego, and the subject was not open to discussion. I had not before opposed him in this way and was surprised when he gave in.

It might have been the next morning or a day or two later—I am not conscious of any time lapse—that he got a man of the rancheria to help him push the Ford back from the barbed wire, kicked the tires and said they seemed all right, measured the gas (at my insistence) and decided there might be half a tankful, gave me a small roll of bills, cranked the car and said goodbye.

The trip to San Diego was as endless, as beset with fears, as confused and nightmarish, as that first trip from Los Angeles to Santa Ynez when I had to learn to drive as I went. If anything, this was worse. It seemed impossible that I would ever reach home, would see my little daughter who perhaps had grown almost beyond recognition, would have the rest and blessed cleanliness which my over-burdened body craved above all else. I determined to drive on all night, not to stop at all (except for gas) till I got there. But in Los Angeles, after dark, confused by the lights and the traffic, I started across a street against a policeman's signal. He motioned violently, and I backed into the car behind me—fortunately not striking it very hard, because by this time everything I did was in slow motion. The policeman came over and spoke harsh words. I gave my license number and home address, and after another severe scolding he told me to go on my way.

For the whole of the next month, as I waited for the birth, I had nightmares, waking and sleeping, about being sued for some impossible sum, about Harrington's reaction, even about being put in jail. I had never had an encounter with the law before. But it is probable that only minimal damages had been done the other car (those were the days when bumpers were bumpers); or perhaps I had looked so forlorn, bedraggled, and poverty-stricken that the driver thought it useless to try to recover anything. Anyhow, I never heard of the incident again, and I never told anyone about it, but suffered through my fears in silence.

Realizing at length that I was in no condition to proceed, I stopped at a cheap hotel in a town somewhere beyond Los Angeles. My room was a windowless cubbyhole, and, being accustomed to fresh air day and night, I felt too stifled and too exhausted to sleep. In the morning I drove on. It still seemed a long journey home. I staggered up the steps, took a long hot bath, and went to bed. My mother burned my clothes in the backyard incinerator.

I never told her how long I had been left alone or how hungry and frightened I had been. I did not want to hear the things she would say about Harrington— and about me for putting up with him. I did say that

I had thought for weeks of the way she used to make creamed salt mackerel as a special breakfast treat when I was a child in Texas. She thought it natural for a pregnant woman to have cravings, and combed the fish markets till she found salt mackerel.

My child by Harrington, a daughter, was born on the twelfth of February. I gave her a name, Awona, derived from an Indian language, one that was euphonious and easily pronounced, before I sent a message to her father. Some of his suggestions had been pretty outlandish.

Harrington wanted me back as soon as possible. His letters expressed affection and said he missed and needed me. I read love where love was not. But somehow I didn't have the courage to drive back alone with a small infant that was still being breast fed. Fortunately, my mother was wild to travel. She had enjoyed our drives in the Ford around San Diego, and she said she had always liked camping out—having in mind, of course, our pleasant, covered wagon trips to my father's Elm Creek Ranch and earlier fishing expeditions to an island in the Gulf of Mexico. She was an adventurous woman at heart, and this offered a vacation from a marriage which after nearly forty years she still found, in certain aspects, distasteful. I, in turn, persuaded myself that conditions in the adobe house might be very different with her there, with the two babies, and all the conveniences we would carry with us. The afternoon of the day the baby was six weeks old we set out.

Since I had been too excited or perhaps too filled with unacknowledged foreboding to eat lunch (even though we had fresh shrimp!), we stopped for an early dinner at the Twin Inns at Carlsbad. There were white linen tablecloths and napkins almost as large as tablecloths, and table settings of blue onion ware. Dignified waiters served platters mounded with fried chicken and tureens of vegetables. The baby slept peacefully under a mosquito net in the car, and her older sister loved every minute of it. Resuming our leisurely pilgrimage, we stopped overnight at a hotel before tackling the Los Angeles traffic. The breast feeding had to be supplemented, but that was just because I was tired and over-excited. The adventure had started well.

Next day even the Ridge Route was fun. We kept passing and being passed by a young couple on a motorcycle, and after a bit we waved companionably at each encounter. It was spring, all the hills were lush with grass and dappled with wildflowers—lupines, poppies, Indian paintbrush, monkey flower, purple and scarlet penstemons, and it seemed a thousand more that I couldn't name. Mother was enraptured. All her life she had longed for spectacular scenery. Although she didn't approve of me, she loved me, and on this trip we were truly companionable.

Then came the inevitabe let-down. I had tried to prepare her for life in the adobe, but it was drearier, dirtier, and more isolated than she had pictured. Both she and Harrington tried to be civil, but found no common ground. I suppose one can say he tried. After a series of rather acrimonious remarks to the effect that on every other camping trip *she* had ever been on, the menfolk made the fire and prepared the morning coffee, he actually got up first one morning and boiled Postum (the kind that imitates coffee grounds) in canned milk. Mother politely declined to sample it, and whispered to me that it was a "gosh-awful mess." Whereupon Harrington drank it with real or pretended gusto.

Our neighbor, Juana, was not different in appearance from the women who had been all around us in Mexico. Her house and person were immaculately clean, and if they could have come together she would have been a solace to my mother. But she had no English and Mother had never learned a word of Spanish. Juana was shy and Mother was still afraid of Indians, at least of north-of-the-border Indians. They never made contact. Once after I had been out several hours with Harrington, I came back to find my mother and older daughter sitting forlornly on boxes outside the door. Mother was trying to keep the child amused while her own spirits sagged. She was not a gregarious woman and did not particularly miss people. But somehow she had envisioned the whole trip as one of sightseeing. She had brought nothing to read, nothing to lose herself in, and she was weighed down by a terrible desolation.

The next morning Harrington planned a quick trip to Bakersfield. For some reason not now apparent he wanted me to go along. He planned on bringing back a load of supplies, including, I believe, a shipment of the precious metal boxes. My mother had a nagging pain in her side that made her willing to forego the long, hot, rough ride, although she definitely did not look forward to being left alone—and at this date I can't imagine why I consented to leave her. Harrington was very bright, rational, and reassuring: we would return in a few hours and he would be sure to bring everything on her list. I nursed my infant. I warned that I might be compelled to miss the next feeding, but would be back long before time for the one after. Her grandmother said not to worry, not to drive too fast, she would give her some of the formula based on canned milk, which seemed to agree with her well.

We made good time. The essential part of our expedition would have been sooner accomplished had not Harrington stopped to chat with everyone involved, but even with these delays we would not have been late in starting back. Harrington, however, was suddenly in the mood for socializing. He looked up first this person, then that one, talking, and smiling, and "making a good impression" with them all. I fidgeted, reminded him of the time, argued that we must go. He became impatient with my impatience. What was the matter with me? We would go one more place, see one more person, it wouldn't take but a minute. As luck would have it, we kept running into people we had known only briefly and probably would never see again. Each encounter was the excuse for another delay. I had given up arguing, which only produced an opposite result; but I had felt my breasts fill and then, ominously, become flaccid. Also, I knew what it was to be alone in that adobe when time passed and nobody came. I pictured crying children, my mother's reproachful face. Suppose the pain in her side got worse? Suppose she was lying ill and helpless on her narrow, folding cot?

At sunset we got underway. I drove as fast as I could up the long grades through the gathering dusk, still absorbed in my frantic reverie. At that moment, relaxed and pleased with the world, Harrington decided to pay me a compliment.

"You know," he announced admiringly, "you're really quite different from most women. They waste a great deal of time in idle chatter, and you rarely ever talk too much."

I answered not a single word. He had wasted the whole day in idle chatter, had brushed aside my pleas, had left a fearful, aging, possibly sick woman alone with her fears and with responsibilities that should not have been hers, had perhaps endangered a baby's health. There was too much that needed to be said. If I began, I should never end. In my bitterness, I felt the premonition that I would never again be able to nurse this child or any other I might have. But along with bitterness, I could feel a hard core of resistance growing within me. It had been a minute crystal when I struck him that first summer in Santa Ynez; it had grown enough to give me strength to refuse to give birth on a dirt floor; and it would grow (though this I was still far from admitting) till it became a wall of stone, separating us forever.

We came to the adobe late at night. Mother had been crying. Her manner was remote and reproachful, making it clear without words that she had thought some accident had befallen us. Her side was much worse. The baby refused my breast.

For many years, I never understood or tried to understand that wasted day in Bakersfield. Now looking back, putting it together with the talks with the Irish janitor in San Diego, and with many subsequent fatuous and seemingly pointless experiences, I begin to understand, I begin to have compassion for a very lonely man, a man whose self-imposed isolation was due as much to a deeply rooted sense of inferiority and alienation as it was to dedication to his work. After all, even his encapsulated personality responded sometimes to a day in spring. On this day he had been away from his informants, from his notes, and from a woman and two small children whom he found nerve-wracking and incomprehensible. He had celebrated by indulging his stifled impulse to gregariousness, excusing himself with the argument that it was always well to "make a good impression" on people whose favor he might sometime need. I do not believe there was ever in Harrington's thought any deliberate cruelty; neither was there ever a trace of empathy or compassion.

Mother's condition did not improve. Two or three days later we put her on the train in Bakersfield. Through the window her face looked old and drawn. She had the baby in her arms, and the older child's face was pressed against the glass, sad with the prevailing sadness. I felt bereaved, torn apart. Only Harrington continued to smile his artificial smile, meant to be an expression of encouragement. Back at Tejon Ranch, he was sure everything would be all right, but gave his word that I would be allowed to drive down to San Diego if we should hear Mother was seriously ill. Meanwhile, all was well. We were alone together, and he could fall back into a good working routine.

For that entire summer, the adobe was our headquarters. Within a week a letter came from my mother saying that she was much better, so I did not go home then; although later in the summer we both went to San Diego for a few days. As I remember it, we also made several excursions to Los Angeles, also a few brief field trips, but most of the summer was spent in the ranchería. It was a busy, learning, exciting summer; but now, in addition to separation from my children, a more intimate distress gnawed at my emotions.

To put it baldly, Harrington considered all available methods of birth control unreliable and artificial. Under no circumstances would he risk curtailing my usefulness by another pregnancy, neither did he wish to forego sex. He found it pleasant and probably thought of it as a way to keep me satisfied and docile. Yet the practice he adopted left me unsatisfied, disturbed, and vaguely guilty. This was long before the mores changed to permit a variety of acts "between consenting adults," years before any public concern over excessive population growth. I did not feel guilty in the sight of God, for I was going through my intensely atheistic phase, but I felt guilt nonetheless—against nature, perhaps, and against the affection we were supposed to entertain for each other. Often I was moody and irritable and thought of suicide, although the life force flowed too strongly in me to permit any serious attempt.

Otherwise, the summer was pleasantly adventurous. Three other persons beside ourselves intruded into the life of the ranchería. Two were "Government men" (possibly from the Bureau of Indian Affairs, on this point my memory is indistinct) making some sort of survey. They were urban, well dressed, sophisticated. In comparison, we were crude and unkempt to a degree, and their manner expressed a definite superiority. When their work was finished, they bemoaned the fact to Harrington that they had no stenographer available. Me they always ignored (they must have thought I was some sort of moron to exist under such conditions), but him they recognized as a man of education, though eccentric. I shocked them by volunteering my services. I could not take notes in shorthand, I explained, but if they would speak distinctly and not too fast I could keep up with them on the trypewriter. Doubtfully, they agreed to try. At first there was a tendency to stop to spell out every unusual word, but when this proved unneccessary, they proceeded normally with the dictation—or rather, one man dictated and the other interposed suggestions. When the work was finished, I offered to make a fair copy. They said my notes were sufficiently clear just as they were. They thanked and complimented me. Later, Harrington said he was very proud of me. I never remember his paying me a compliment on my appearance, but, if I happened to do anything that showed skill and intelligence, it pleased him highly, especially if others were impressed.

The other visitor was a blond, very Nordic young man with (in the summer of 1917!) a thick Germanic accent and equally thick glasses. He was making a study of rattlesnake venom. He wore high, heavy boots and had an undisguised fear of the snakes he set himself to collect. I have forgotten his real name. The Indians called him *El Viborero*, the Rattlesnake Man, and that was the way Harrington and I spoke of him.

Tousled, disheveled, and shabby I might be, but I would never again be as dirty as I had been the preceding winter. My baths might be "spit baths," taken in the small tin washbasin, but I was determined that my clothing should be clean within reason. That core of independence was slowly growing. I insisted on having my washing done, since I had no facilities for doing it myself. Harrington did not protest too strenuously. After all, this might afford an opportunity for me to become acquainted with some of the women of the village.

The woman who consented to do our washing was a gracious, friendly matron who already had a grandchild or two. Harrington suggested that I ask her if she knew any "Coyote stories." As she sat placidly mending my underwear (a service for which she would not accept remuneration), I brought up the subject of myths in my halting Spanish. *"No conoce ud. unos cuentos? de Coyote, tal vez, en el tiempo cuando los animales eran gente?* (Do you not know any tales? of Coyote, perhaps, in the time when the animals were people?)"

My friend proved curiously evasive. I persistently returned to the question on several long hot afternoons, sitting on the porch in front of her little frame house, the wooded hillside sloping gently down before us and rising steeply behind. She was courteous but reticent. Yes, she finally admitted, she had heard of such tales. The old people probably remembered them. Yes, possibly she had even heard some of them. But no! she could not repeat them to me, she could not tell me anything at all about them, because it was not *el tiempo* for telling ancient stories. I was puzzled. The lazy afternoon seemed to me an ideal time for story-telling.

On one such occasion, her four-year-old grandson, amusing himself by hopping over the rungs of a ladder that lay on the ground in front of the house, stepped on a baby rattlesnake. It was a very small rattlesnake, but then it was also a very small child.

Pandemonium broke loose. The child's mother, whose presence up until that moment I had scarcely noticed, screamed that he would surely die. Someone ran to find *El Viborero*. That red-faced and frightened young man rose to the occasion. He put a tourniquet on the child's leg, made two timid, shallow incisions across the wound and sprinkled it with permanganate of potash crystals. He did not attempt to suck out the venom—I think none of us had the guts to do that.

I persuaded them to let me drive the boy to *el doctor* in Bakersfield. Harrington was located, and was amenable to the suggestion. He saw it as an opportunity to solidify our position with the people of the village. I did not understand till many years later, and possibly he never did, that in the mind of the People the child had been bitten because I had forced them to think of subjects that were forbidden in the summertime. Fortunately, they were a kindly and tolerant folk. Perhaps they did not hold it against me because, being a congenitally stupid white woman, I was innocent of evil intent.

We set out in the Ford, Harrington and I in the front seat, the mother, child, and *El Viborero* in back. The little boy, wrapped in a quilt and cradled in the arms of his wailing mother, was obviously very sick.

At frequent intervals, carefully timed by *El Viborero's* watch, we stopped to allow him to loosen the tourniquet for a brief and also carefully timed interval. The child's father (or putative father) did not accompany us. Later there was enjoyable gossip in the ranchería. It was whispered that now suspicions were confirmed. The woman's husband was not the child's real father. Had he been, he would have refrained in accordance with ritual from drinking water while the boy's life was in danger; he would not have dared to go on eating and drinking as usual.

At three o'clock in the morning, under the harsh lights of the treatment room I watched while the doctor slashed the wound deeply, deeply, and induced profuse bleeding. Others might look away, but I would not, although everything swam around me. I don't remember what else was done. At last the doctor said not to worry; the child would be all right now. He said the tourniquet had probably saved his life, and *El Viborero's* treatment had been good, as far as it went; it would have been better if someone had sucked the poison out. I was given bandages and medication, and told that the wound should be dressed daily for two weeks. This I faithfully did, perversely enjoying the unfamiliar and uncongenial Florence Nightingale role and enlarging my circle of Indian friends.

In all that time spent at the Tejon Ranch, that strangely idyllic time in spite of all the fear and unhappiness that it contained, I do not remember a single rainy day. Rain must have fallen, perhaps while I was in San Diego, for when I brought my mother there at the end of March the slope below our adobe was freshly green. One morning shortly after she had left, I opened the door on such whiteness that for a moment I thought the snow I had so dreaded in my time of loneliness had made a belated appearance. All the downward tilting land was covered with popcorn flowers that had opened overnight. They dazzled the eyes in the morning sunlight and freshened the air with such a faint honey-fragrance that one could not breathe enough of it.

The popcorn flowers soon vanished. Spring became high summer, and all the open land was covered with the pale brown, sun-parched grass that is the usual clothing of a California hillside. But one more drama was to be played out upon that slope. One morning we saw a tide of black toiling slowly, inexorably up it, like some mysterious blight. It proved to be an all but endless army of stinkbugs, *pinacates,* those unpleasant, largish insects which, when menaced, stand on their heads with their sharp posteriors elevated; and which, when crushed, emit an unbelievably loathsome stench. Hours later, reaching the adobe, the insect horde did not divide but proceeded up the walls, climbing a few feet awkwardly, falling back, and trying again. They came in at the door, and those that were swept out turned around and came back or were immediately replaced by others. They clambered up the inner walls, and fell with disgusting plops into whatever was cooking on the stove. They interpenetrated everything, even the metal boxes. Harrington had already formed the habit of squirreling away bits of food, usually stale cheese or dry bread crusts, in these boxes along with his notes. Long after the invasion had passed, we found in one of these almost airtight containers a honey-combed piece of cheese and several dead stinkbugs.

IV The Draft Threatens, And Fieldwork

FOR ALL THE work he knew he was accomplishing, Harrington was not consistently happy during that spring and summer of 1917. He was a congenital worrier, incapable of more than momentary flashes of contentment. He worried about being recalled to Washington, about being forced to publish prematurely, about someone else publishing similar studies before he did, about another ethnologist stealing his informants, about his expense accounts being called into question. After the United States entered the war and it became evident that he would be required to register for the draft, he became the victim of a very specific dread, the intensity of which I was slow in realizing.

Discussing the matter as we drove down to Los Angeles, he told me to pull off onto a side road, he wanted to talk to me seriously. He then proposed that he should lie down, extending one leg, and that I should run over it, crushing it thoroughly. He would recover, he argued, being lame would not seriously handicap him in his work, but would make him forever unacceptable to the army. This was a lonely place, out of sight of the highway. Now was as good a time as any to get it over with. I tried to laugh the suggestion off as a bad joke, but he was entirely in earnest. When I vehemently and tearfully refused, he tried to exact a promise that if worst came to worst and he actually was drafted, I would cooperate in some such scheme to save his life.

I didn't know about such things. I thought it unlikely that he would be drafted, or if drafted, sent to fight in the front lines. A man of his talents would surely be more useful as an interpreter or perhaps as a translator of captured documents. And I must admit that in a secret corner of my mind I thought I would not be unhappy if he should have to serve in the army for a while. He would learn to straighten his shoulders and carry himself well, and he would wear a uniform. (I was young enough, silly enough, to think that rather delightful.) I would live at home and receive an allotment, and boast about my husband in the armed forces, being then equal to the daughter of the people who lived next door to my parents, who was forever talking about her husband the captain. Of course I did not want or expect anything to happen to Harrington. But I dreamed that just possibly, if the pattern of his experience was entirely changed, our life together would be the better for it.

Harrington's thoughts were entirely different. If physical incapacity, the best and surest grounds for exemption, could not be achieved, then the next best pretext would be to present himself as sole support of a family. At that point he decided we should drive on down to San Diego to make the previously mentioned visit. He had a very serious talk with my father, asking if it would be all right with him if he listed both little girls as dependents. My father agreed. After rather grudgingly paying for my confinement, Harrington had, up to this point, assumed no responsibility even for his own child. My father believed no doubt that from this time on there would be regular contributions, but such was not Harrington's intention. To him, "claiming responsibility" and "being responsible" were two entirely separate concepts. My father was a man who bent over backwards in matters of financial obligation, and it took him a long time to understand that his daughter was married to a man who lived by different standards. Long afterwards, when my mother had come to accept divorce, in spite of the implied disgrace, as inevitable under the circumstances, she was to speak of Harrington, a man who could beget a child and make no provision for it, as no better than a tomcat. I understood her point, but considering his perverted Puritanism, I thought a tomcat was not an apt comparison.

We did, however, have these few rather happy days together in San Diego. The baby was rosy and thriving, and already, of the two children, very much my mother's favorite. She had reached the noticing stage, and it seemed rather sad she reacted to me as to a stranger. Harrington tried to pretend an interest, but it was all obvious and awkward sham.

During this visit his genuine interest, aside from arriving at an agreement with my father, was in having my mother make a money-belt for him. He specified that it should be of very heavy canvass (too heavy almost for Mother's foot-treadle sewing machine), cross-sewn into compartments, with buttoned down flaps—quite an undertaking, and one which tried her patience sorely. Harrington had become as fearful for his money as for his life, and was determined to withdraw it from his savings account and to carry it on his person for the duration of the war.

At the time Harrington had asked me to maim him, I had asked, "Why? Why would you rather be a cripple than go into the army?"

"Because I don't want to die," he explained, "I can't afford to risk getting killed."

"Everybody has to die sometime," I argued tritely, "Lots of things are worse than dying."

"Nothing is worse than dying," he returned. Then added with a heartfelt emphasis that I had never heard in his voice before, "I would rather be sick, blind, in prison, and undergoing daily torture than be dead."

"I wouldn't," I shuddered. "What would there be to live for?"

"I could still *think*," he answered, "It would be terrible not to be able to think."

Harrington had clearly stated what was for him the ultimate horror. Although I was untrained in philosophical reasoning, it seemed to me to have a ring of falsity. If death was, as both of us then claimed to believe it to be, the complete extinction of the personality, how would one know he wasn't thinking? And not knowing, how could he be hurt? I did not advance this argument. My companion's statements had been so strongly felt that I caught a momentary vision of him sick, blind, in prison, tortured, still persistently mulling over words he had recorded, analyzing, coordinating, reaching ever more far-fetched conclusions as he became farther removed from reality.

About the time of this conversation, Harrington began to rail long and frequently against Christianity, because, he said, it was a religion of death. He objected to the cross as its central emblem because it brought to mind the death of Jesus, and he also objected to the doctrine of reward or punishment in a life beyond the grave, simply, so far as I could gather, because those teachings forced one to face the inevitability of death. In regard to an afterlife he, like me, professed to be an out-and-out unbeliever; but, as will be seen, this disbelief was capable of being shaken. The subject was distasteful and he did not wish to dwell upon it. Christian ethics pro or con did not enter into his consideration of the religion. His ethic was expediency, and I doubt if he was sufficiently developed in this area to grasp the ethical teachings of any religion.

At the Tejon Ranch, after, I think, the ordeal of registration, there was a death in the Indian community. We were invited to the wake—I don't know whether they called it a "Wake" or a "Cry," for I can't recall either the Indian or Spanish word applied to the ceremony. Harrington insisted, much to my embarrassment, that I go alone. He said he had stomach cramps. Since his stomach not infrequently did give trouble, rebelling against spoiled food or too much food eaten in order "to save it," I accepted his excuse. Later I wondered if the cramps had not been brought on by his aversion to anything associated with death. I went, dutifully if timidly, and found the event friendly, solemn but not, in its overall effect, depressing. At intervals, we, the mourners, feasted on such meager fare as the village afforded: tortillas, refried beans, jerky stewed with dried and pounded chile peppers, all served with side dishes of chiltepeñas, miniature red peppers hot as live coals; and naturally gallons of coffee. Outside, wearing their stiff, broad-brimmed felt hats as they stood around the fire where coffee boiled, the men of the ranchería gravely passed around a bottle, returning to the house for food and worship with undiminished dignity though ever more uncertain footsteps. A man who was said to be able to read a little read or at least repeated in a somewhat garbled way passages from a Spanish prayerbook. He held the book before him, but did not actually appear to look at it. As the night wore on, four very ancient women seated on the ground with their backs against the wall wailed ritually for the dead. There was a definite rhythm of eating, listening to prayers and wailing. This ritual wailing was the most authentic, the most impressive part of the ceremony. It bridged untold centuries. I have since wondered that there were no songs for the dead, no dances. Perhaps they had been forgotten, for it is unlikely that they had never been. The people of this ranchería had been Catholics for a very long time.

Harrington was interested in all that I had to tell him and instructed me to make a record of everything that I remembered. Maybe after all his stomach cramps had not been psychosomatic.

We left the ranchería for other fieldwork in widely scattered places. Mostly, I remember this period in disconnected flashes: an ancient, almost blind woman wiping her streaming eyes with a moleskin, explaining that, because of its softness, moleskin was very good for sore eyes while I silently worried about germs; another woman, old but vigorous, chiding me because I persisted in tasting as well as smelling every plant I brought to her for identification. *"Que muchacha!"* she said, *"de repente tu vas a comer veneno"* (What a girl! One of these times you are going to eat poison.) Then again, memory covers a complete episode.

There was, for example, our expedition to a ranchería high up in the mountains near the headwaters of the Tule River. As was frequently the case, it was made without proper preparation. We set out one morning from whatever town was our headquarters, leaving our clothing and most of our food supplies behind. Because the distance wasn't far on the map, Harrington thought we could drive up there, see what the prospects were for gathering information, and then come and go at will. We found, after leaving the highway and beginning the real climb, that the road—if that is what it could be called—was truly horrendous, a track that could be negotiated by a sure-footed horse, or with difficulty, by a muledrawn wagon, but entirely too much for the Model T. It was used to rough treatment, but nothing like that. This road was filled with small boulders and jagged outcroppings of rock, and the gradient was incredible. Finally our engine stalled and would not start again. We were thoroughly stuck, unable to turn around, and in a situation where backing down was beyond my skill.

Apparently, there was nothing to do but leave the car. Harrington was unwilling to abandon his fieldtrip, I was for hiking back the way we had come. Before we could come to an agreement, we heard another Ford chugging away below us. It rounded a sharp bend and the driver caught sight of us and came to a stop. A man and his wife were going deer hunting, far up in the mountains. They were well prepared, even to having provided a length of pipe which could be screwed into the opening of the gas tank and filled with gas to increase the pressure. (It will be recalled that the gas tank in the Model T was located beneath the front seat and gas traveled to the carburetor by force of gravity; if the gas fell below a certain level on a steep grade—or even when the tank was full if the car was too steeply tilted—no fuel reached the engine.) Even with this added piece of equipment, even with the wife doing her best to push, the road was proving too much for the new arrivals. They assumed we too were on a hunting expedition, and Harrington let them believe this was true. Of course we had no guns in sight, but they probably thought they were wrapped in the canvass bedroll on the backseat. They eagerly proposed that we join forces, and Harrington as enthusiastically agreed. I could drive, the other woman couldn't. The front seat cushion was removed from our car, the pipe screwed in place, and tank and pipe filled to the brim from one of the extra cans of gas the other couple carried. I sat flat on a board and drove while the other three pushed. After a few yards had been gained, we all walked back to the other Ford and repeated the process. This went on, again and again, through hours of blistering heat. Then came a stretch of road where each car could proceed under its own power, and there were even occasional places where one could turn off. We saw the scattered houses of the ranchería. Harrington directed me to pull to one side and let our friends pass.

"This is as far as we go," he told them cheerfully.

They reacted with incredulity, outrage, and dismay. They said we couldn't hunt on an Indian reservation, and wasn't the plan to go up to such-and-such meadows, higher up the mountain? At last they pleaded: wouldn't we at least help them get where they were going? The road was probably bad again further up, maybe even worse than what we'd just got over. They might not make it alone. On the other hand, if we would help them we could come back here, if here was where we really decided we wanted to stay; it would be downhill all the way.

Harrington refused, almost casually but quite definitely. He would not even discuss the matter. Later he commented, "They seemed upset." He was both bewildered and slightly amused by their vehemence— he just couldn't understand why people would get so worked up over anything as inconsequential as a hunting trip. I don't think he offered to pay for the gas that we had used or even thanked them for their help. This was one occasion when he felt under no compulsion to make a good impression.

Having now arrived at our destination with such difficulty, there would be no running back and forth to a base of operations. We must stay on and make the best of what we had, or rather, what we hadn't.

These people were not too friendly towards intruders. Most of them spoke some English, and they had English names. They had never been missionized; in fact, in the days of the missions, they had not infrequently harbored runaways. The medicine man, Tom, spoke against us. In spite of this opposition, Harrington found a satisfactory informant. About the only food we had was several boxes of cereal, which, probably by inadvertence, had not been removed from the car. I complained, but for Harrington the richness of the information more than compensated for the poverty of our diet. Someone reluctantly sold me a little rancid grease so I could fry slices of the everlasting "polenta" to make it slightly more palatable. It was said that Tom had told them not to sell us food, and besides, they had little to spare.

The stream roared ceaselessly through a gorge it had cut in solid rock. Beyond it the mountains rose abruptly, covered lower down by dark forest and capped by stark granite. On our side, there was a little sloping cleared space backed by more dark and rugged mountains. The houses of the ranchería were scattered at random about this meadow or hidden among the encroaching trees. Here the sun rose late and by three o'clock in the afternoon all was in shadow.

At first I ran wild in the forest. I chewed pleasant tasting manzanita berries to allay the pangs of hunger, and once, having fashioned primitive equipment from a stick, some twine, and a bent pin, I actually caught a small fish. I used part of it for bait, but when it became evident that there were no more where that came from, I broiled the remainder on a stick held over a small fire. I felt free, reckless, strangely happy. I bathed in an ice-cold pool at the foot of a small waterfall. The water in the pool was neck-deep, swift as well as cold. It took me off my feet and I didn't know how to swim. Nothing made any difference, nothing frightened me. I hoped I would meet a bear in the woods. I was only shy of people, but Harrington felt that I should be supplementing his information. I remember talking to an old woman who was winnowing grain on the hardpacked threshing floor. Talking to is scarcely an accurate way of putting it, for she had little if any English and possibly less Spanish. But we communicated after a fashion. The light was fading, and she was roasting a woodrat for her evening meal. She gave me one of the minute hindquarters, and I never tasted anything so delicious.

Then I became well acquainted with a couple named Henry and Anna. I believe that this was after Harrington had set me to gathering plant specimens for future identification and securing their Indian names. Anna was possibly my first paid informant. I frequently ate my noonday meal in her home. Anna had lost her sense of smell. She could not tell whether the beans she had put up from her vegetable garden were spoiled or not. By that time I preferred the risk of botulism to starvation.

Neither Anna nor I was particularly interested in an endless series of plant names—I wonder where among Harrington's effects the dust of those forgotten specimens is scattered, for I think it highly improbable that they were eventually preserved and given their proper botanical names. We dawdled and talked of many things, and some of what Anna told me I can never forget.

There was a woman, she said, unhappily married to a worthless man and despised by her companions. She and the other women were gathering seed right there in that very meadow, but because of her ostracism she was working a little apart from the others. That was when the mythical Bear carried her away. Having brought her to his home in a cave in those inaccessible granite crags, he assumed the form of a handsome young man. They lived there together for a year, then he returned her to her home, pregnant with his child. She never saw her bear-husband again. But now her human husband's shiftlessness was no longer a reproach to her, for at frequent intervals she would find a deer or other game laid at the door of her house. We spoke often of this story, always as of something that had happened long ago. Then one afternoon when Henry came in from his field, Anna demanded, "Show the woman that you are a son of the Bear." Henry demurred, his wife insisted. With some embarrassment he rolled up the sleeve of his shirt and showed me, high on his forearm, a patch of approximately a square inch in size where coarse longish black hair sprouted from thick skin. This was the proof that the wife of the Bear had been his remote ancestress. It was the mark that all her descendants bore.

I do not know if these people had the taboo on

telling myths when the snakes were not dormant. Probably they did. I think Anna told me this story because it was not actually an ancient tale. In her mind it was a factual link between prehuman beings and the world of men.

Along the rocky banks enclosing those rushing, relentless waters there was said to be a deposit of a poisonous substance that had been used by the ancients. In one of my semi-suicidal moods I inched my way across the face of a boulder that bellied out over the stream. There was a precarious trail on the surface of the rock, chipped out and enlarged from natural footholds. I found and tasted the "poison," which proved to be alum, broke off a bit to take to Harrington so he could secure the Indian name and the proper terms for its taste, texture, etc., then gingerly returned as I had come. I had not really believed that there was poison at the end of the trail, nor had I really wanted to take a fatal fall.

We stayed in that remote and magical place for at least a month. Harrington made one trip down by wagon with an Indian and brought back some meager supplies. "I remembered to bring your butter," he said, proud of his show of consideration. But the butter had melted and run away in the heat of the slow journey.

During all this time I dreaded the return of the couple who had gone deer hunting. One reason that I hid myself so much was that I was ashamed to face them. But we never saw them again nor heard of their passing. They must have found another route, for if an automobile had gone by the ranchería it would certainly have been noted and commented upon.

Returning from this Tule River expedition, or perhaps from another equally protracted, we visited the Southwest Museum to pick up our accumulated mail. I was particularly anxious to hear from my family, for although I may have sent a letter or two out I had not received any for a long time. Harrington told me to stay in the car, he wouldn't be a second, and he didn't want to be delayed in starting for wherever it was that we were going. The sun went down. I fretted a little but I knew how his seconds were likely to stretch.

It was almost dark when he came back. Even in the gloom, even from a distance, I could tell from the way he carried himself that something was wrong. He came up and gripped the car door tightly. He was not quite crying, but terribly shaken. He said, "My mother died." I took his head in my arms and comforted him as best I was able.

I seem to recall having met Harrington's mother once, briefly. At any rate I have the impression of a rather large, rather domineering woman. Perhaps she was not actually large physically, but only seemed so in comparison to her amiable little cricket of a husband. I think it was she who transmitted to her older son his intelligence and intellectual ambition. Certainly she and not the father had been mainly responsible for forming his character. She had no doubt had to manage carefully, both in her New England home and when they were getting a foothold in California. She certainly impressed upon her children the righteousness of penny-pinching and the utter immorality of anything savoring of waste, luxury, or extravagance. I knew that Harrington respected her, but until her death I had not realized how close the tie had been.

I don't remember that he attended her funeral; perhaps it was already over.

Don Juan, the *brujo,* during the process of initiating Carlos Castaneda into the realm of "non-ordinary reality," defined twilight as "the crack between the worlds." It was at twilight that Harrington told me of his mother's death; and it was at twilight a few days later that he came into the smoky glimmer of lantern light, white and trembling, even more shaken than on the prior occasion. (My unreliable memory insists on locating this scene on the Tejon Ranch, although I do not actually think that was the place.)

At first he could only gasp that something dreadful had happened. He didn't want to say what it was.

When I pressed him, he admitted in tones of utter horror, "I saw my mother."

I held him as one would a distraught child. Then I said carefully, surely with a wisdom beyond my years, "I don't believe you actually saw *her*. You are over-wrought, you have been thinking about her a great deal, I believe you just saw your own thought, your memory of her."

He could only shake his head and shiver.

Then I asked, "Did she ever harm you while she was alive?"

"No," he said, "never."

"Then, assuming that there is some kind of life after death and that you really saw her, why should you think that she wants to harm you now? What would have changed her?"

The light of intelligence came back into his face. He emerged almost visibly from the cloud of superstitious dread. Now he was thinking again, and he was safe.

"No one ever talked to me like that before," he said.

I had performed correctly in my role as comforter. But it was a shallow comforting, not based upon any real sympathy for Harrington's very real fears. Although I prided myself on rationality and materialism, that stubborn, unregenerate area of my thought which insisted upon self-knowledge was maintaining all along that I would have given my eyeteeth to have seen a specter.

More and more frequently I found myself assuming the motherly stance recommended in Lummis' despised and discarded letter; the trouble was, I had no maternal authority.

V   Life Styles And Tensions

EARLY IN OUR time together Harrington showed me some of his poems. This was perhaps his greatest moment of self-revelation. He handled them reverently, like a medieval man uncovering the relics of a saint. I was appropriately awed and praised them beyond the point of honesty. It was not, however, that I was being intentionally hypocritical; I knew my own taste in poetry to be unsophisticated and I assumed that anything this superior man might write could well be beyond my ability to appreciate. I then spoke timidly of certain poets, and may even have suggested that we read poetry together. Harrington explained that it would never do for him to read poetry. He intended to become an outstanding poet, and a poet must be, above all else, original; if he read poetry that someone else had written, he might unconsciously fall into the error of plagiarization.

Of his poetry I have only the impression that its movement was, like his own bodily movements, awkward. Only two things do I recall his doing deftly and with grace: true up a manuscript so that the edges of its pages were beautifully even, and wrap a secure and tidy parcel. I admired these skills——because to this day if I attempt to put a manuscript in order the last state of it is worse than the first, and all my parcels are disasters.

One thing is certain. His poetry could not by any chance have contained the twin themes of love and death, foundational to most poetry; because he could not feel love nor bear to contemplate the thought of death. It must also have been lacking in color.

While I waited in San Diego for the birth of our child, we exchanged frequent letters. Mine must have been genuine love-letters, for I was still, even after the vicissitudes of the Tejon Ranch, an extremely sentimental young woman. Now a loveletter by its very nature demands poetry. Once I quoted some lines from Kipling: "O fountain in the wilderness!/ O cistern in the waste!/O bread we ate in secret,/O cup we drained in haste!" And on another occasion I included a verse by Joaquin Miller: "Hark to the song of the dove, my love, Of the dove in the ripening wheat;/ There are many tomorrows, my love, my dove,/There is only one today." I think I still had hope of persuading my husband that we might fill our days and tomorrows with other things beside the correct transcription of dying languages. I reasoned to myself (though I would not have dared say it to Harrington) that the people who spoke or had spoken these languages had also existed as human beings, had lived and loved and felt. Harrington took no notice in his answering letters of these scraps of poetry. When we were reunited I asked if he had liked them. They were well enough, he supposed, but what did they *mean?* To him, he said, they were meaningless. And he asked again to be spared exposure to what others had written.

I was also to learn that we differed radically about what constituted proper poetic comparisons. One afternoon we were driving west toward a particularly marvelous sunset, a great area of smoky rose shot with flame below a clear, faint band of green. Both of us commented on its beauty. Then I ventured to describe it as "opalescent."

Harrington was furious. I had rarely seen him so angry. How could I compare a beautiful natural phenomenon with an artificial thing like a gem? He was continually amazed at my shallowness and artificiality.

I was too taken by surprise, not to say crushed to make the obvious response: that opals occur in nature. I thought of my little ring put away at home, a fire opal surrounded by seed pearls, given me by my parents on some birthday in my early teens. I thought with inward weeping (for I no longer wept so often outwardly) of the many gentle, lovely things which I had once thought to be quite innocent and now was painfully learning to be unmentionable. I wondered what comparisons I was to be permitted to make and what forbidden. I no longer believed Harrington's opinions to be invariably right, but I wished to avoid his anger and especially his sulking. On this occasion he did sulk, for at least two days, letting me feel the full weight of his displeasure over my bad taste and blatant artificiality.

There was, however, an occasional episode which made me wonder even then (and more in retrospect) whether his glorification of a "primitive" (i.e., squalid) way of life was not more than a simple rationalization of a never outgrown resistance to order and dislike of washing and whether his anger at what he called artificial and others might term beautiful or gracious or merely normal might not be a case of the proverbial sour grapes, a deliberate working himself up to despise that which he felt to be out of his reach.

Take, for example, the time in the first or second summer of our marriage when we drove an informant over the vast Irvine Ranch in the attempt to locate some Luiseño Indian sites which he thought he remembered. The informant is faceless and formless to me, but he must have been there, because our lunch of bread and cheese and bologna, eaten as we sat on the ground under the sparse shade of a sycamore tree, was accompanied by a bottle of wine—the cheapest claret, sour and thin as watered-down vinegar, but a lovely color. All was bright and pleasant till we packed up to resume our drive. Then we found that one wheel of the car was stuck in the soft earth and only spun itself deeper when I tried, alternating between "drive" and "reverse," to pull it out. Harrington was crouching down trying to dig it out with his bare hands (we never carried proper tools) when a man approached on horseback, an assured, well-groomed man riding a beautiful horse and thoroughly conscious of his superiority.

He said something sharp to the effect that "you can't camp here. Couldn't you see this land is posted?" He may even have added a contemptuous, "Can't you read the signs?"

Harrington, red-faced and filthy, looked up and met the horse-man's eyes. There was a moment of incredulous recognition, accompanied by sheer horror on Harrington's part and a look of startled amusement in the expression of the other man. They called each other by name. Harrington, not introducing me, explained that he was engaged in ethnological research. The rider murmured with barely suppressed laughter that it was perfectly all right, but he really should have spoken to someone at the ranch house—gesturing vaguely over the hill—since if some of the hands had found him they might have handled him roughly for trespassing. Couldn't let just anybody wander over the property, you know. He then offered, with that same half-contemptuous, easy condescension, to send a man to help us. Harrington muttered that we'd get out all right by ourselves. With a casually lifed hand, the other man rode away.

"Who was that?" I asked.

Harrington repeated his name, which I have long forgotten. "We were at Stanford at the same time," he said. "I barely knew him. He was a fraternity man, I was a student." An even darker tide flooded his face as it crumpled into a petulant, exasperated grief. "Why," he almost wailed, "why did he have to see me digging like a gopher?"

That involuntary cry of distress called up a vivid picture of the contrast between the unconsciously arrogant rich man's son, enjoying all the amenities of university life, and the dull, shabby grind, stumbling awkwardly over menial tasks that must be performed to eke out his scholarship, spending every spare penny on books and every spare moment in study to satisfy that compulsive, over-powering thirst for knowledge. Harrington was even then a driven man. He was doing primarily what he wanted to do. Yet there must have been sternly repressed pangs of envy for a life of ease and power and pleasure, sternly repressed shame at the drab and clownish image reflected back to him from the eyes of the fortunate and the cruel. This may account in part for his obsessive desire to "make a good impression."

I understood even better the drab graceless facets of Harrington's nature after we paid a visit to his family in the Simi Valley. This took place in December of 1917 or 1918—most probably the former, but at any rate after Mother Harrington passed to her reward.

Perhaps erroneously, I seem to have gathered from Harrington that his parents were traditionally more rationalist than religious—as native New Englanders, they may have leaned towards Unitarianism. Be that as it may, the younger brother, Robert, and Ethel, his wife, were very religious. They had named their little daughter Bethel (there were also one or two boys, all very young, very close together—I don't remember that the boys' names had scriptural connotations). Since they belonged to some strict fundamentalist sect, it may have strained their principles to celebrate Christmas at all. But celebrate it they did, after their fashion. In the living room an immense Christmas tree (which would doubtless be sawn up for firewood later) reached from floor to ceiling. Its sole decorations were walnuts wrapped in bits of foil that Ethel had saved up. No lights, no tinsel, no popcorn or cranberry festoons, no candy canes, no anything except those dreary, ill-disguised walnuts.

The whole house was damp, chilly, and uncheerful, although Ethel rose before everyone else each morning with an air of determined martyrdom to light a fire in the kitchen and another in the living room. No number of fires could have mitigated the emotional chilliness of that household. Ethel must have sprung from stock every bit as thrifty as her husband's. All the unsaleable eggs, the "cracks," "peewees," etc., she put down in a solution called "water-glass." This preserved them, but imperfectly. At breakfast the main dish was always scrambled eggs, because they could be prepared in no other way—it even seems to me in retrospect that we had them at every meal, but that is too much, that surely could not have been. The whole atmosphere was gray, a grayness accentuated and aggravated by that great un-Christmas-like tree and those piles on piles of sickly pale yellow, gray-tasting eggs. The children had colds and whined a good deal.

I remembered the Christmas seasons of my childhood, not always happy because my parents sometimes chose that time to quarrel violently, but always colorful and exciting—perhaps in the monotony of life in that tiny, mid-Texas town all holidays shone with a peculiar brightness. The Christmas tree, put up several days before the Holy Night, blazed with bright ornaments saved and added to from year to year, and candles, not often lit before Christmas Eve and carefully watched by my mother, who had reason to be afraid of fire. The preparation of food began days before the tree was up. At that time and in that place only poor white trash celebrated the season with less than twelve cakes. My mother labored for hours over the ones that had to be fresh-baked—the fruitcakes, particularly the dark fruitcake had been made and stored away "to ripen" months in advance. Every afternoon for weeks before Christmas she made Christmas candies, preparing the fondant, coloring, shaping, and decorating it to satisfy her artistic taste. There were only the three of us, we were not gregarious, and except for an occasional visiting cousin there would seldom be anyone to share our feast. But portions of cake and boxes of candy would be taken to those households with whom we maintained a sedate, non-intimate social intercourse, and sometimes to the less fortunate. The cake might be reciprocated in kind, but no one ever tried to make candy like my mother's.

The feasting at our house began before Christmas and continued at least through New Year's. For our lighter holiday meals we had, among other delicacies, calves' brains scrambled with (strictly fresh) eggs, fried oysters, or cold snacks of "pressed chicken" between slices of homemade bread. For dessert we had ambrosia and preserved fruits and puddings; and almost everything, including the cakes, was drenched in whipped cream. Christmas morning my mother somewhat reluctantly agreed to have my father invite his crony, "Old Man Paddleford," the second stingiest man in town, in for eggnog. Not being accustomed to liquor, Mr. Paddleford usually got mildly tipsy, and my mother, with an angry sniff, would threaten not to have him in the house again.

Here in Harrington's childhood home, there was no feasting, no cake (or at least none that I recall), no candies, homemade or otherwise, and assuredly no eggnog.

We did manage one evening of something that might have passed for mild gaiety. Ethel brought out a book of familiar songs, which I played very badly on the piano while the others sang. Once, suddenly getting the hang of a tune, I quickened the tempo and left everybody behind. No one laughed. There was general embarrassment and I apologized. For God's sake! We were *young* and 'twas the season to be jolly; yet everyone seemed to be preoccupied only with not making a mistake. True, there had been a death in the family, the dominant member of the household was no longer with them, but I sensed no pall of grief.

At the close of this dreary visit, Harrington went about his business. I believe he collected some notes he had left at the Southwest Museum and went on to Washington—this is certainly the case if the time was 1917. I drove "Old Man Harrington," as my parents referred to him, to San Diego to get his first glimpse of his newest grandchild. I liked Harrington *père* very much. He seemed to be just emerging from a repressive shell, he was certainly no mental giant, yet he was kindly and he could laugh. As usual, the trip seemed to take an unconscionably long time, and as was not unusual, after dark I got lost. We took a wrong turn, several wrong turns, and wandered in and out of Camp Pendleton, which was ahum with suspicion and military activity. Everytime a lighted sentry box loomed up out of the fog, we were challenged, with varying degrees of harshness, and turned back. Grandpa Harrington and I shared amusement at being taken for possible spies or saboteurs, but we were very glad indeed when we finally came out on the right road.

At our first meal at home, my mother decided that she did not like my husband's father any better than she liked my husband. "He licked his knife," she complained, "and then stuck it in the butter." Mother was never backward in letting it be known that she had the squeamish stomach proper to a lady. At the next meal, she laid her well-polished silver butterknife alongside the butter dish, but Mr. Harrington ignored it. I don't know what my father thought of his co-grandfather; it is certain that the two men found no common ground.

I don't remember Mr. Harrington's actually being there for Christmas, but he probably was. At any rate, I stayed on for a while after his departure, preparing for my first trip to Washington. During this visit my mother remarked to me, privately and in a whisper, that the child born in wedlock obviously had "better blood" then the child born out of wedlock. Despite the way she phrased it, her conclusion had nothing to do with blood or inheritance. It was based on the mystique of matrimony and on the fact that the younger girl was prettier, more clinging and gave promise of being more biddable than her precocious and self-willed half-sister. My mother disliked all she knew of the Harringtons, and, because of them, had formed a poor opinion of all "old New England families." Yet she had liked the father of my older child well enough up until the point where he decided that, since my father had less money than he had assumed and was not inclined to part with what he did have, it would not be to the advantage of a well-established bachelor to saddle himself with an idle, spoiled child-wife.

Now I come to a conflict between a deep, instinctual impression that tries to pass itself off as memory and the loose and uncertain chronology which I have attempted to work out. I find myself recurrently besieged by the thought that Harrington and I were together in Santa Fé and its environs before we were in Washington. This notion may be due in part to the vast amount of material on the Taos language that Harrington had with him in Washington, and which, immediately upon my arrival, we began to work over together. But this material may well have been gathered shortly prior to our meeting in that period of his somewhat ambiguous association with Hewett, about which I know so little. And I ask myself, if we did go to New Mexico before we went farther East, how and when did this happen? We did not drive there, for the Model T was never driven outside of California. If we went by train, surely my first long train journey with Harrington would have contained enough bizarre and embarrassing incidents to make it unforgettable. New Mexico was not a stop-over on my first trip to Washington, for I recall that trip in great detail. Nonetheless (perhaps simply because on this earth New Mexico lies between California and the nation's capital) in the terrain of memories so old they have become dreamlike my first fragmentary New Mexican recollections seem to have a place prior to the Washington experience; therefore, I shall insert them here and not later, where they almost certainly belong in order of time.

For a few days at least we stayed in Santa Fé. Harrington took me to see the Museum of New Mexico and we went to dine with Dr. and Mrs. Hewett. Their dining table was a slab of polished cedar, a single cross-section cut from a tree of incredible antiquity. Also I seem to recall a little Mexican or Indian maid, summoned by the tinkling of a silver bell in the hands of our hostess. All else is virtually blank—I hear the faint sound of voices but do not remember a single word. This one evening terminated our social relationship with the Hewetts, because we never reciprocated a courtesy. Our living quarters were invariably unsuitable for entertaining, and Harrington would have been no less ashamed than I to have a caller enter them; also, in his opinion, only informants rated a free meal.

It was as we walked along a street in Santa Fé that Harrington told me he had had an offer from some college or university in California to teach linguistics and ethnology, and that the offer included financing for summer field work. Immediately, while he was just beginning to explain the proposition to me, I saw my lost and longed for Academia, constructed surely of the self-same stuff as the towers of Camelot. I saw ivy-covered buildings (derived unconsciously, no doubt, from the expression "Ivy League"), and a quiet campus where dignified professors and eager students strolled together, mutually dedicated to the pursuit of learning; and most important an adjoining, tree-shaded street, and on that street a white house, *our* house, with an ample lawn in front of it where two little girls in starched white dresses played amicably. (Who would keep the house in order? Who would tend the lawn? Who would wash and iron the children's clothes? The dream-maker does not concern oneself with such details.) Caught up instantly, like St. Paul, to the seventh heaven in this waking vision, I spoke —and managed to say precisely the wrong thing.

"We would have a settled place to stay," I said. "We could have a house of our own and a lawn for the children to play on."

"Lawn" was the triggering word. He would never, Harrington said, live in a house with a lawn. A lawn was an artificial thing. And didn't I know that children should play in the dirt? *In the dirt!* That was the proper, natural way to bring children up. Children were little primitives and should be brought up in a primitive manner.

He fumed on and on, beating a dead horse, while I, as usual in such circumstances, could say nothing effective. I might have commented that his own child at that very moment, providing she had been able to escape her grandmother's over-protective arms, could well be playing on a reasonably well-kept lawn. What was the use? I finally admitted to myself what I had long known but refused to acknowledge, that for as long as I lived with this man I would have no place where it was possible to keep my children with me.

The subject of a teaching position was never again mentioned between us.

It is my impression that we moved in a few days to Taos Village, already beginning to be known as the home of artists and writers. It was situated about two miles from Taos Pueblo proper, where strangers were not permitted to stay.

I remember sitting in the livingroom of a neat little house in the midst of an alfalfa field. I was talking to a young white woman about my age who was married to an Indian from Taos Pueblo. Harrington had gone somewhere with the young husband—for what purpost I now have no idea, possibly to try to run down a potential informant. The young wife had two plump, pale brown babies, and another was expected. She remarked that Tony was always glad to pick up an extra dollar, because they had been having a hard time lately. Tony, she said pridefully, had been offered a good job, but it would have involved being away several days at a time, so of course he had had to turn it down.

"Why?" I asked in all innocence.

The girl looked at me with an expression that was a comment on my stupidity. "Because he wouldn't think of leaving me here alone overnight," she said.

I thought of my weeks alone in the adobe on the Tejon Ranch. This Tony had given up his birthright, his citizenship in the Pueblo, to marry a rather nondescript young woman; yet he still cherished her to the extent that he would not leave her alone overnight. I had then to admit another fact of life; namely, that I had never known a husband's protective love.

Taos Pueblo lifted its structured reddish-brown heap against the sky, continuing symbol of man's labor and aspiration. It might have stood there forever, habitation and fortress, raised by the hands of people armored in exclusiveness. I viewed it with awe and fascination, but always from the outside.

Harrington had an interesting tale to tell of the first visit to Taos of a pioneer woman ethnologist, Mrs. Matilda Stevenson. It appears that this rather formidable lady did not travel light. She brought with her bags and cases of various kind, as well as a sizable trunk. "Take all my things inside," she ordered the man (possibly an Indian) who had driven her out to the Pueblo. "I always live among the people I am studying," she added when he began to protest. The man tried to explain that no strangers were allowed inside the Pueblo overnight, that even a son or daughter of the People who had married a member of another tribe could never again spend a night inside. Mrs. Stevenson overrode him. He shrugged and obeyed. The Indians of Taos watched impassively while the white woman's luggage was unloaded. The driver departed. At the hour of sundown strong hands carried bags, boxes, and trunk outside, then firmly though without unnecessary roughness placed the lady herself outside the walls. The redoubtable and distinguished ethnologist was left sitting alone on her trunk in the swiftly falling dark and increasing chill of the New Mexican night. Harrington's story left her there, inferring that she spent the night alone with her belongings. Mrs. Stevenson died, I believe, shortly before I went to Washington; but Harrington had known her well, and she was said to have had a soft spot for him in her gallant heart.

Harrington was, when the spirit moved him, an interesting conversationalist. We did sometimes still have pleasant times together, especially when the subject of our talk dealt with his work or with people he had known in connection with it. But I no longer accepted his every word with wide-eyed wonder. As my knowledge grew, some of his theories began to sound untenable, if not actually weird. He thought, for example, that there were far too many separately classified linguistic stocks. He even proposed that all the languages of North America (or at any rate of the American west) could be categorized at "Patlan" or "Atlan," according to whether or not their word for "water" was *pa* or some variant thereof. I don't know if he ever committed this theory to paper, or simply talked it out in endless conversations.

The informant whom Harrington finally secured (I believe he had worked with him before) was named

Manuel. He was a dour, silent man with black braids framing his dark face and falling down over the immaculate white sheet in which he draped himself. His moccasins were always impeccably whitened. He had little rapport with Harrington, even less with me. He answered questions with great deliberation, and, I am sure, accurately, but he volunteered very little.

VI The Company
        Of Scholars

AT THIS DATE, I have no idea what Harrington's salary
was. Indeed I may never have known precisely, because in certain matters, especially money matters, he
was always secretive, even with his wife. Of this I
am sure: according to present-day standards, it must
have been minuscule. He bemoaned his inability to
put money aside after marriage as he had done before,
even when working for next to nothing. It seemed
two could not live as cheaply as one. Also, there was
the added expense of the purchase and maintenance

of the car, and, after I became sufficiently trained, of my informants. These he paid almost entirely out of his own pocket, since it was virtually impossible to finagle salaries for two informants at the same time. Later, on top of all this, there was the typewriter. Now that he had a typist, Harrington became obsessed with the idea of a machine upon which Indian languages could be written with the degree of phonetic accuracy which he demanded. After literally years of correspondence on the subject, he located a company which made a Russian language machine and would replace the Russian alphabet with the English, plus those characters and symbols which he required. It cost, for that period, an enormous amount of money, over four hundred dollars, I believe. I don't recall its being in his possession before early spring of 1919; which meant, as will be seen, that I actually had very little opportunity to use it. (Many years later his daughter kept it for him for a long time, during which she typed some of my manuscripts on it.)

I must mention that I had a small private income, two hundred dollars per annum, paid in two installments. This came from dividends on bankstock that my father had placed in my name shortly after I turned sixteen. When it became evident that Harrington was not interested even in supporting his own daughter, I hung onto this money, although the honorable thing to do, as I very well knew, would have been to turn it back to my father to reimburse him in part for his expenses in providing for the children. The idea also occurred to him, and once only he made the suggestion to me. But before the words were fully out of his mouth, my mother flew to my defence. She did not approve of my conduct and way of life anymore than he did, and in matters of importance they frequently talked things over and reached an agreement on what to do for me or about me, but on occasion she could not resist assuming her old role of the brave mother standing between me and the "cruel" father. Truly my father was anything but cruel, except occasionally to "soulless" animals. He used to say sadly that "all young'uns took to" him except his own daughter. Feeling so strongly the physical dissonance between my parents, and identifying with my mother, I always pulled back. Now to a certain extent my little girls gave him the affection I had withheld. He never resented the children, but he did resent and totally fail to understand Harrington's stinginess. For my part, I had gradually become so thoroughly indoctrinated with my husband's view of his work and his money that I even at one time spent a hundred dollars (half my yearly income) on a Graflex camera to use in photographing informants and placename sites. I also remember purchasing with my own money a loosely woven flat basket for leaching acorn meal and a watertight basketry jug, both immensely old. Now at the turn of the year my check arrived and I used it to outfit myself for Washington.

Harrington had not led me to infer that we would have a sedate but reasonably active social life in Washington; he had merely let me infer it. Just as he had let the deer-hunting couple assume that our destination was the same as theirs. I do not believe that he was always intentionally devious in such matters. It is my understanding that he instinctively allowed people to continue in whatever view would make them happy and assure their maximum cooperation. One might say this was his way of assuming the protective coloration that would enable him to avoid conflict and pursue an uninterrupted train of thought.

I remember telling my mother that I would be going out frequently during the coming months. We shopped accordingly. We bought readymade a very respectable gray suit and chose material for two "good" dresses, which she would make up for me at home. The one I liked best was a rather stiff silk, a taffeta, I think, with a geometrical design in dark blue, black, and white. I rejected pinks and reds as unsuitable to the dignity of my position; and although I would dearly loved to have chosen some shade of green, I did not dare because of the furor caused by my purchase of the green hat. I wore this hat when I went downtown with my mother, but feelings of resentment and defiance replaced the sharp, fresh joy that had accompanied its purchase.

One day in the preceding summer, in an inland valley town, probably Bakersfield, we had parked the car and Harrington had gone one way and I the other to make certain purchases. After I bought my groceries, I passed a shop window completely filled with apple-green felt hats of various shapes and sizes. Incredibly, they were on sale for a dollar apiece! The color enchanted me. I had always loved the fresh green of spring and, when very young, had entertained a fantasy about being married in green. I had made some good buys on groceries and had a dollar to spare.

I chose a rather small hat with a brim that could be turned back from the face. In the mirror, under the magic green hat, my cheeks were very pink and my eyes sparkled. I had the salesgirl put whatever dreary thing I had been wearing in a bag, picked up the paper sack full of groceries and started slowly back to the car, pausing to look at my reflection in various shop windows. It did not trouble me at all that the bright new hat was incongruous with the rest of my well-worn and not too clean clothing. I had parted amiably from Harrington; in fact, we had been getting along rather well for several days. I felt a surge of desire to show him myself in the new hat. For a long time I had been dull and without any sense of youth; now I felt foolishly girlish.

Curiously, I find it hard to write or even to think of what came next. Up to a point, I remember it in detail; then there is an interval that is blocked out except for the after-shadow of hurt and shock.

I came upon Harrington standing on the sidewalk, talking to a man I did not know. The stranger's back was towards me. I came up gaily, but before I could say anything, Harrington caught sight of me. A most peculiar expression flashed across his face. He scowled briefly, shook his head, then with an air of forced geniality, went on with his conversation. I stood there, stupidly embracing my bag of groceries and the parcel containing the old hat. After a moment I moved to one side to make myself part of the group. Harrington moved too, blocking me off with his body from his companion's view. I should have walked on past to the car, but I continued to stand there, not knowing why I was excluded from the conversation and growing angrier by the second.

Finally there were the usual amenities, nice to have seen you, etc., and the other man went on his way, glancing at me with a moment's faint curiosity.

Harrington turned on me. I cannot remember at all what he said, except that it concerned "that thing" on my head, and did not include the usual charges of extravagance and artificiality. Indeed, when I tried to explain that the hat had cost only a dollar, which I had saved out of the grocery money, he most untypically implied that it was not the money but "the principle of the thing" that he objected to. What principle? I never knew, I never even had an inkling. To this day I fail totally to understand his reaction to the green hat, and particularly to my wearing it in public. I do know that if I had walked down the streets of Bakersfield stark naked, he could not have been more offended, more completely outraged and revolted.

I took the hat off and put it in the paper bag that had been given me for my old one, but I did not destroy it. I kept it hidden among my possessions till such time as I could take it out in my parents' home, try to remove the creases (fortunately, it was a soft felt) and wear it on the streets of San Diego. I wore it off and on for years to come, but never again in Harrington's presence. From this point on I found no difficulty in acknowledging that I was happier in Harrington's absence though for a time yet, after each separation, I hoped that things would be better when we were reunited.

Early in January of 1918, I was ready to leave for Washington. The Ford had been driven into the garage, and someone had been hired to put it up on blocks, remove the tires, and drain the radiator and crankcase. The day before I left I stood looking at the poor, deactivated thing, sitting there like an impaled bug, and a wave of nostalgia swept over me, not so much for what had been as for what might have been. Unwisely, I tried to express this to my mother, without actually betraying the whole of my feelings.

I said, "I feel rather sad at leaving the car. After all, it is the nearest thing to a home I've had during my entire married life."

"That," she replied with a vigorous sniff, "is plain silly. Who ever heard of feeling sentimental about a car! Now if you felt bad at leaving your children, that would be a different thing."

I did feel bad at leaving my children, but there was no use trying to convince my mother. She always deplored my sentimentality, which she rightly assumed I inherited from my father. After more than forty years of marital incompatibility he still liked to tell little sentimental stories about their courtship and early married days, stories which my mother demolished with a few cutting words.

I was, however, happy and excited about the trip to Washington, buoyed up by the perennial hope that, once I had arrived, everything would be different. I was going to join my husband, and this gave me points over the girl next door. She had given birth to a boy about the time my younger daughter was born, and her soldier husband was now in France. She stayed home with her child, as my mother never tired of pointing out, although she couldn't very well have done anything else, and in her case, as in mine, the grandmother assumed most of the care of the infant. The girl next door idolized her husband, pined for him, lived from one letter to the next, and she and her mother frequently consulted an ouija board to ascertain his whereabouts and state of health; while I could claim a husband, a distinguished scientist, who was safe in the nation's capital and eagerly awaiting my arrival.

Poor girl next door! Her captain became a major and she was justifiably proud of him. But when the war was over he did not write nor come to her for a long, long time, and when he came, it was only to look briefly at his son and to tell her that he wanted no part of her forever. Quiet and broken-hearted, she did, as always, the genteel, the proper thing. She went to secretarial school, got a job and an apartment, and made a home for her little boy. There on a day some years later, when the child was visiting his grandparents, she took out the service revolver that her husband had given her for her protection in the first year of their marriage. She put the muzzle in her mouth and pulled the trigger. Yes, she was "nicer" than I, "more ladylike," and never, till that last desperate moment, did she cause her parents to bow their heads in shame. But I was tougher. Indubitably tougher. Certain of my rough, thoroughly undesirable pioneer ancestors had bequeathed to me the instinct for survival.

Since Harrington had drawn his money out of the savings bank, I, too, was given a sum to carry on my person—a comparatively small sum, never more than three hundred dollars. From this I was empowered to take my traveling money, the implications being that I would employ the utmost economy. But I did not. I took a lower berth in a Pullman car.

The government had taken control of the railroads and passenger traffic was a shambles. We progressed from one siding to another, where we sat for hours on end, waiting for troop trains or watching them rush past. It required five days to go to Washington, D.C., from San Diego, via "the Southern route." There was no dining car service, and we always seemed to make our stops where there were no restaurants in the railway stations—or, for that matter, no railway stations. At intervals the butch passed through, hawking his unappetizing wares: cheap magazines, and, in the way of food, peanuts and candy bars, tepid soft drinks, and now and then a few stale sandwiches.

I shared my ample, home-packed lunch with a young woman about my own age. The sardine sandwiches, the turkey sandwiches, and the deviled eggs wouldn't have kept long in the stuffy car. The fruitcake was more durable, but we ate it up anyway. I admired this girl's sophistication, her hair style, the way she dressed and spoke. She had quit her secretarial job in New York, drawn out her savings and made a trip to California, frankly husband-hunting. Now, disillusioned, she was homeward bound. I had a husband, and in his absence I could dilate upon his good looks, his intelligence, his superior education, and important job. That evened things up in a way.

At our end of the car there was a disparate group of people who clung together during the journey like members of the same family, then parted at its end never to communicate again. One was a master sergeant. He had been stationed for many years overseas and I had the impression that he was now to be assigned to some camp to assist in the training of recruits. He was a man of enormous girth, with a red face, stentorious voice, and domineering manner. With him were his wife and a couple of children, teenage or a little younger, mother and children all so colorless and quiet that I remember them only as dim bodies orbiting around the man of strength. Another woman returning to her home in New York, of uncertain age and definitely less respectable than my secretary friend, worked industriously at crocheting an elaborate toilet seat cover with a fringe of small woolen balls while she bragged about her "wonderful boyfriend." During our interminable waits, the butch often stopped to chat, sometimes exchanging risque jokes with this woman, which the rest of us pretended not to hear. The porter, too, when he was not busy, tended to stand on the edge of our group. He had the wisdom and tolerance of a man who had worked as sleeping car porter for many years. Patently disgusted with the deterioration of service, he discreetly kept his mouth shut most of the time. Now and then he could give a little information about our rate of progress or when we might reach a place where food would be available. I felt a rapport with this man. I told him I was unused to traveling alone, asked him to look out for me, and tipped him something each day, less to buy his goodwill than as a silent expression of my own.

The rest of the car was occupied principally by young men in uniform. They were alternately boisterous and depressed. At night they and other service men from elsewhere on the train shouldered their way up and down the aisles, many of them in various stages of inebriation.

At New Orleans we expected to get food; instead we were marooned all night long on a siding outside the city. A few hardy and well-heeled souls took cabs into the city to eat and sleep in hotels. This was risky, for no one could say just when the train would be on its way. When I was ready to retire, the porter took a sheet and fastened it securely inside the curtains of my berth, making a double screen between me and the aisle. No one else got such attention. In the morning, the secretary reported that she had been "scared half to death" all night by soldiers attempting to invade her berth. The crocheting woman said she had been approached and ardently solicited by the butch. "I should put out for him, when I already got a wonderful boy friend! And for nothing, yet!"

At long last we were told that there would be a twenty minute stop and food waiting for us in the railway eating house (the equivalent of a western Harvey House, but I don't believe it was so called) at Montgomery, Alabama. That was still hours away. The porter told our group confidentially that there were so many soldiers to feed we just might not get anything for ourselves. He named a very good restaurant a short distance from the station that was sure not to be crowded. "Of course," he said, "it's up to you folks." Just in case, he gave careful directions. Well after dark, the train pulled into the station. The master sergeant (together, naturally, with his family) opted for the railway restaurant, and so did the woman with the toilet seat cover. The secretary and I, younger and more adventurously inclined, decided to take the porter's advice. We stood at the entrance of the car, determined to be first off when the train stopped, since we were afraid of not making it back in time. Pushing our way out of a station jam-packed with service men, we ran hand-in-hand through the narrow, darkened street. (I'd swear they were cobblestoned, but that must be a memory from Mexico.) Counting the intersections, we made what we agreed must be the proper turn and sighted a dim globe of light, painted black on top. "This must be it," we said, and opened the door with considerable trepidation.

We stepped into the ante-bellum South. The red carpet was worn thin in places, the crimson velvet drapes had their shabby spots. But there was nothing shabby about the white linen tablecloths, the heavy, gleaming silver, the fine china; and especially not about the magnificent waiters in evening dress: dignified, solicitous, respectful, aloof—beings from another century. There were only a few other diners. Although our rumpled, travel-worn appearance did not match the elegance of the establishment, we had prompt and undivided attention. We explained that we had to get back to our train without delay and immediately large, old fashioned soup plates filled with gumbo were placed before us. This thick mixture of rice, okra and chicken was a meal in itself. Then there were fat, piping hot fried oysters, and the fried chicken, and I don't know what went with it, for by that time we were too stuffed to notice side dishes. We looked at our watches, passed up dessert, which we couldn't have eaten even if there had been time, and ran, panting, back to the station.

The train hadn't left and didn't get underway for quite a long time. The master sergeant, chewing a toothpick, told us we had "lost out." "I had a steak so thick," he boasted, measuring its thickness between his own thick red thumb and forefinger. We knew we had not lost out. More than a meal, we had had an Experience.

By morning the train definitely had become a local. Between the inevitable waits on sidings, it now jerked itself slowly up through the Carolinas, stopping and starting again at every way station and even at places where there was only a signboard. At these brief stops, one or two people, usually black, would get off and walk away down some narrow red dirt road or along what looked like a cowpath into the woods. We were all hungry again, and weary. Everyone else fretted over the delays. In a curious reversal, each stop became to me more like a reprieve. The emotion I had tried to disguise as anticipation was showing itself with increasing clarity as apprehenson.

Harrington was waiting for me. When I saw him, my heart sank rather than leaped. He was glad I had got there at last, changed his impatient frown into a forced smile, gave me a peck and a brief hug, and strode on ahead through the crowd. But facing the heavy traffic outside the station, he grasped my arm hard and thrust me before him like a shield. He had never done this in Los Angeles, although he had always expressed some fear of traffic. In Washington he was higher strung, partly, no doubt, because he was unhappy at being there. His time was not his own, he was exposed to the human contacts which rubbed him raw, he was oppressed by the terrible need to get out of this prison and back to informants who might not even be alive when spring came. I don't think he ever actually reasoned that if a car was going to strike someone, better me than him. He just instinctively grabbed the nearest object (me) and held it in front of the oncoming threat.

Within ten minutes we had quarreled. A short time later I was ensconced in my Washington home: a second floor apartment, small bedroom, and slightly larger combination kitchen and dining-room, with communal bathroom at the end of the hall. This apartment was in one of a row of conjoined red brick houses with front steps and iron handrails. These had once been respectable private residences; now the area was no better than a slum. This address would never be given out, for Harrington no less than I would wish to hide the shoddiness of his living quarters. Here the wives of his colleagues would never come to call. Here I would never give small dinner parties nor entertain "little gatherings" of interesting people. I observed cracks in the wall and ominous stains on mattress and bedding. Luckily, while in Mexico, I had learned how to deal with bedbugs.

Harrington explained to me how Washington had originally been laid out in four sections. He knew the whole story of the designing and building of the city. Although on certain subjects, most notably on anything to do with human relations, he had such blind spots as to appear stupid, he had a phenomenal memory and a far greater fund of general information than I was ever destined to accumulate. That was why, when conditions were right, he could be a brilliant conversationalist. Many years later his grownup daughter visited him in Santa Ana, California. His appearance had become so seedy that she was ashamed to be seen with him; but she rejoiced in their long nighttime rambles, when the darkness mercifully hid him from sight and his talk sparkled with all sorts of interesting items. Now he told me that the southeast part of town (where we were to live) had deteriorated and become unfashionable or even unrespectable. Most of the scientific community, he said, had their homes in the northwest section or out in the suburbs. But what was the matter with this place? It suited our needs precisely and it was cheap. And why did I want to be a snob?

The street in front of our rooming house was filled from one side to the other with sharp-edged ruts of dirty gray ice. The sidewalk was slippery as wet glass except in those spots where a more self-respecting or civic-minded householder had sprinkled ashes. I seldom went out without at least one fall. There must have been a few other lodgers in the house with us, and there was certainly a landlord on the first floor, but I retain no memory of any of them. I passionately detested the whole milieu and blotted out as much of it as possible.

On the other hand, I fell in love with the castle-like Smithsonian Institute and with the snow-covered mall in front of it, where squirrels wearing thick and elegant winter coats scampered in bare-branched trees. The rose window in the old building particularly appealed to my romantic nature. I loved to look at it from the outside and was fascinated by the patterns of light it cast on the floor of the room behind it. It seems to me that Harrington's office was situated there, but I could be mistaken on this point. Virtually every weekday, I worked faithfully in that office, a diligent, unpaid secretary, trained to meet my employer's needs. I also toured rather hurriedly the exhibits which the building housed, but this was the extent of my Washington sight-seeing. Time was not to be wasted.

I can remember sitting in Harrington's office typing, but I cannot remember what I typed. Surely we must have made a pretense at least of putting the Chumash material in order, since most of his vouchers had been made out for paying Chumash informants. At home we worked exclusively and almost frantically on the Tanoan material. Harrington bought a roll of butcher's paper, which he meticulously divided into sheets that would lie nicely on our combination kitchen and dining table. On these sheets he diagrammed all the ramifications of the Taos pronoun: the various pronominal postfixes in combination with free standing forms, also with verbs and nouns. I never quite saw the sense of these oversized diagrams, for they contained nothing that could not be shown on sheets of ordinary writing paper. But Harrington enjoyed making them—it was about the nearest he ever came to having fun. Ultimately, he had a stack approximately six inches high. Before I left Washington I pulled the stuff together and wrote a paper on "The Taos Pronoun." With amazing generosity, Harrington presented it for publication under my own name, and Dr. J. Walter Fewkes, Chief of the Bureau of American Ethnology, accepted it. I believe I was even paid something. The number "twenty-five" comes to mind, but whether I received twenty-five dollars or produced twenty-five pages of stilted and incomparable dullness, I couldn't say. There must still be copies filed away in musty archives.

Both Dr. Fewkes and his wife were kindly people. Harrington claimed to despise Dr. Fewkes as elderly and pedantic, and ridiculed his overwhelming interest in the Hopi and particularly in Hopi kachinas, but then Harrington had always to bolster his own wavering ego by feeling superior to everyone else. When Harrington introduced me to the chief, he immediately asked for our address so that Mrs. Fewkes could call and welcome me to Washington. Harrington made some lame excuse about having a temporary place only. Dr. Fewkes was doubtless skilled in dealing with human oddities. He probably guessed that Harrington had stashed me away in a place that he was ashamed to have anyone visit. A few days later we were invited to dine with Doctor and Mrs. Fewkes at their home in Forest Hills, Maryland.

As a matter of fact, we dined there twice, and the second time, because of some inclement weather conditions or failure of transportation, we stayed the night. Of the first occasion, I remember most vividly my excitement during the longish interurban train ride. I wore my silk print dress and was thoroughly infected with Harrington's anxious desire that I make a good impression.

Mrs. Fewkes was a devout Christian Scientist. During our second visit, as I helped her make up the bed Harrington and I were to occupy (such clean linen, so fresh, so white!), I happened to remark that I had recently been in bed two days with a cold and fever. She fixed me with a firm but kindly gaze and stated, "You were resting." Both Harrington and I found this excruciatingly funny. I was young and crude, and association with Harrington had improved neither my manners nor my humanity. I saw nothing improper in laughing at a kindly hostess. My own Christian Science phase was years in the future.

Dr. Fewkes' only comment on his wife's religion was the already timeworn judgment that it was all right, but it was neither Christian nor scientific, always uttered with a kindly twinkle that took the sting out. But Harrington claimed at great length that the old gentleman had been unduly influenced. He blamed Mrs. Fewkes for her husband's failure to secure obviously needed dentures and a hearing aid. He also insisted that the true name of the Hopi was *Mukwi,* but that *mukwi* meant "death" or "dead," and therefore Mrs. Fewkes had persuaded the Doctor to refer to them always as Hopi, said to mean "Peaceful People." It is true that certain tribes call the Hopi *Mukwi,* but I have not heard the word translated as having anything to do with death or dying; and the question arises: why would the Hopi (or the Mukwi) docilely accept this rechristening?

Harrington also objected to the use of the word *kiva* to designate the underground place where Pueblo men conduct certain religious ceremonies. For some reason he preferred the Spanish *estufa,* employed by some of his informants. To him *kiva* was an artificiality for which he blamed Dr. Fewkes.

One social function Harrington was eager to attend was a testimonial dinner for the eminent ethnologist, Miss Alice Fletcher. I am not quite sure whether this was given during my first or second visit to Washington, but I clearly recall Harrington's excitement. I naturally would have given anything to go, but had to resign myself to staying home when informed that Miss Fletcher would be the only woman present. Harrington rented evening clothes for the occasion and purchased a dress shirt. He neglected to purchase cufflinks, but in those days women sometimes wore shirtwaists with starched cuffs, and I had a pair. However, there was nothing we could do about studs. He attended the dinner wearing the plastic studs that came with the shirt.

Afterwards I asked, "How was Miss Fletcher dressed?"

"Same as the men," he answered, "black with something white in front."

It was definitely during my first stay in Washington that we were invited to dine with Miss Fletcher and her companion of many years, Mr. Francis LaFlesche. When Harrington was given the address, he really felt he had it over me. "Look at that!" he crowed, "Miss Fletcher isn't ashamed to live in the old part of town." He couldn't see and never did see the difference between living in one's own home, probably inherited, certainly loved and well kept up for many years, and renting two rooms in a vermin-infested slum.

Francis La Flesche was, like Harrington, employed by the Bureau of American Ethnology. He was a full-blooded Omaha, middle-aged, and heavy from years of city living, but still a fine figure of a man. A certain female clerk at the Bureau, trembling on the verge of confirmed spinsterhood, was said to have cast sheep's eyes at him, but I never heard of his responding. He had been associated with Miss Fletcher for many years, first as informant, then protege, finally collaborator.

The house they shared was indeed old, and perhaps a little over-furnished in the Victorian way, but it had a lovely atmosphere, a *comfortable* atmosphere. Miss Fletcher was elderly, full-figured, pale, mentally alert. She was diabetic, and Mr. La Flesche watched over her diet with an eagle eye. We ate, I remember, a delicious roast, but I believe there was no dessert. Mr. La Flesche explained that Miss Fletcher could not eat sweets.

I have of their joint work only a few hauntingly beautiful songs, translated by Miss Fletcher from the Omaha.

Harrington had another Indian colleague in the Bureau, a Huron (if I remember correctly), a sluggish type who had not gone into the field for years and had no desire to do so. He published, however. I seem to remember the texts of myths with dull translations which shifted into Latin whenever they promised to become interesting. His name is a blank to me.

Still another colleague whose name I do not recall was a short, red-faced, balding man who held the theory that life in America tended over the course of several generations to make the descendants of all immigrants dolicocephalic, no matter how round-headed their ancestors had been. As I was learning, this man and many others who devoted themselves to the pursuit of science tended to evolve fantasies into theories and then to find or twist facts to support them. The first question put to me by this anthropologist was how long had my people been in America? When I replied, "Five generations," nothing would do but that he must get his calipers and measure my head immediately. To his disappointment, I was brachycephalic. In fact, he found me excessively, inordinately brachycephalic, more round-headed than anyone of my ancestry had any right to be. I remembered that my father's head looked rather long, my mother's decidedly round, and I refrained from telling him that I had been a stubborn baby who refused to sleep in any position except on my back.

The measurer of heads had as his hobby the collecting of butterflies. He must have had a thousand specimens from all over the world. When he described with what I thought too much gusto the method of impaling a living butterfly, I protested its cruelty. He then explained patronizingly that butterflies did not have a complex nervous system and were incapable of feeling pain. To me his specimens still represented a thousand minute crucifixions.

Harrington had taught me a French verse, the plaint of Mary Queen of Scots: *"Adieu, charmant pays de France,/Berceau de mon heureuse enfance."* I once quoted this to the man with the butterflies and the calipers, apropos of what I don't remember, probably showing off on some very slender pretext. He simply looked blank. Harrington said nothing at the time, although when we were alone he told me that my accent had been perfect and that his snobbish colleague had merely pretended not to understand. I believe that at times Harrington was deeply embarrassed by my lack of academic background.

Harrington's resolution neither to read nor to hear poetry did not extend to that fragment of French verse. He thought it surpassingly beautiful and frequently repeated it aloud as he paced around the room or went about some mechanical task, such as cutting up his roll of butcher's paper. He claimed to speak fluent French and German, and without doubt his claim was true. Yet apart from the abortive attempt to have me learn Russian, he neither encouraged me nor gave me time or opportunity to learn any foreign language. He taught me the French verse as one would teach a parrot, and he sometimes discussed French pronunciation in a very sketchy way. Also, he discoursed on the German system of word-building, comparing it to certain American Indian languages and explaining, for example, that in German "thimble" was *fingerhut,* finger-hat. But he never undertook the task of transforming me into an educated, let alone a cultured person; he merely molded me into a competent assistant.

Miss May S. Clark was headclerk of the Bureau, I believe. Whatever her actual title, she held a position of considerable importance and had held it for many years, taking dictation in old-fashioned Pitman shorthand and typing out letters and reports by the hunt-and-peck system. She was a small woman with wrinkled, rosy cheeks and bright, dark, birdlike eyes; intelligent, practical, yet with an underlying strain of mysticism. What she saw in me I'll never know, but we became fast friends and our friendship endured until in her last illness she became too feeble to keep up the correspondence. She was well accustomed to dealing with eccentrics and took Harrington and his ways in stride. However, after we came to feel at ease with one another, she confided that she had found Harrington's expense accounts unique and somewhat puzzling. She had been particularly intrigued by the recurrent item: "Boiling beef for Indians, 5 lbs. @ 5c per lb.—25¢." I never quite admitted that this beef had usually been for our nourishment, not the Indians, supplementing the ever-present and frequently half-sour pot of mush.

Miss Clark invited us to dine and spend the evening at her neat little surburban home. She had lived there with her mother, and sometimes in remembering that first year in Washington I seem to half-sense a frail, elderly presence. But this, I think, is illusion; I believe the mother had already died before I arrived in Washington. At any rate, this was one invitation that was repeated at intervals, since Miss Clark was undeterred by our failure to reciprocate. Harrington was never loathe to accept. He did not begrudge the time, for he felt that he was cultivating a friend at Headquarters—and there was always the lure of a free meal.

On a bitterly cold night we went to visit a group of Kiowas who were in Washington on official business for their tribe. Harrington said it was our opportunity to contact authentic Plains Indians. He was so enthusiastic that I shared his excitement. The Kiowas were housed in a hotel that had seen better days. It was now a combination of fleabag and firetrap, catering to Indians with little money to spend. We walked along the narrow, smelly, dimly lit hallway with its threadbare red carpeting, and knocked upon a certain door. Although our visit had been prearranged, the response was so slow in coming that it seemed as though we were not to be admitted. At last the door was opened. We entered a hot, musty room where three or four Indians sat draped in blankets. Harrington took out his basic questionnaire and proceeded to ask for certain words in the Kiowa language. Responses to these questions and to all attempts at conversation were so deliberate as to make it appear that the speakers lived in another time-world where a day was as a thousand years, or at the very least two seconds were as five minutes. Even the words were spaced out, with gaps between words and also between syllables. The answers, if one had the patience to listen for them, were coherent and intelligent, but always interminably drawn out. An hour of interviewing produced almost nothing. After we left, Harrington said the Indians had been under the influence of some drug, probably, he thought, peyote.

Rounding out the record of my much anticipated social life, I should mention that Harrington took me to call on C. Hart Merriam. I have in mind the picture of a rather short, very erect, very vocal and opinionated man with scarlet face and gleaming white hair, and, I think, a white mustache. I remember the huge maps on the wall of his study and the voices of the two men in earnest, animated conversation on a topic about which I recall nothing. Merriam was one of the very few men whom Harrington did not denigrate. He was rumored to be a great eccentric, and that may have made him a kindred spirit. Also there was no doubt about his not being a Jew. (Of course, Dr. Fewkes was obviously non-Jewish; but he was advanced in years and Harrington privately and for my ears alone characterized him as "doddering" and "bumbling.")

On Harrington's lips the word "Jew" always had a pejorative connotation. I had known this ever since the day early in our association when he had mentioned his reluctance to consider me as a possible wife until he had determined my racial origins; but only here in Washington did I grasp the depth and bitterness of this prejudice. He thought all Jews were perfidious, and cited many incidents to prove his point, of which I remember only one. This was wartime Washington, full of suspicions and rumors. Harrington said that a Jewish colleague of his had been dismissed from the Bureau of American Ethnology for subversive activities, only to be rehired a few days later by another department of the government to translate highly sensitive documents—an illustration, he said, of both Jewish deviousness and bureaucratic blindness, if not outright crookedness. This was Harrington's version; probably the man had merely been transferred to a position where his linguistic talents would be useful to the war effort.

(I wonder where Harrington stood in World War II; I wonder what he thought of Hitler. Perhaps his official biography will clarify these points.)

Harrington was convinced that every linguist, every ethnologist, Jewish or non-Jewish, but particularly the former, was devoting time and effort to securing a glimpse of his (Harrington's) fieldnotes. By the same token, he devoted much time and thought to plotting some way to get a look at *their* fieldnotes. Once only (to my knowledge) he succeeded and he never confided to me the means of this dubious accomplishment. One day when I had not accompanied him to the office he came home early with a slim folder of someone's unpublished notes (Edward Sapir's I think. Sapir was a brilliant ethnologist of whom he spoke often and enviously). These notes must be copied immediately, Harrington said, whispering even in the privacy of our apartment and trembling with excitement. I promptly set to work, and when I had finished he returned the manuscript to whoever had conspired with him or to whatever drawer he had lifted it from.

I remember no single word of what I wrote. But *if* the notes were Sapir's and *if* they had to do with the

Southern Paiute, this was the most important single event of our stay in Washington. For if my perhaps unjustified assumptions are true, the sight of this material may well have sparked Harrington's decision, a little more than a year later, to send me to Parker, Arizona, to work among the Chemehuevi Indians; a decision which eventuated in our permanent separation and turned my life into an entirely different channel.

Winter lingered on into months which should have witnessed the beginning of spring. Miss Clark and others said brightly that the weather was "unusual." (Prior to this I had thought that only California had "unusual" weather.) They said we were "having a regular New England winter" and that "most years we have an open winter." I didn't believe a word of it. I could not picture Washington except as a sort of purgatory of dirty ice and dirty snow. Then almost overnight the snow was gone, the trees in the mall were covered with fresh green leaves, the squirrels had their summer coats, and Negro women dug basketsful of dandelion greens from the grass.

Soon beds of tulips glowed everywhere. I thought them the most beautiful flowers I had ever seen, probably by contrast to the prolonged dreariness of winter. But now, almost without transition, it was high summer when by the calendar it should still have been spring. Tempers flared in the sudden, oppressive heat. Across the courtyard from our kitchen a black woman leaned out an open window and reviled a man on the ground beneath, and he shouted obscenities back. It was worse than winter. Then one could at least go into a heated room to escape the cold, now there was no refuge from this humid torment.

In this month of May, Harrington was champing at the bit; but he couldn't get away for another month or more—probably some question of appropriations. Since I was now thoroughly grounded in the Taos language, he felt I was prepared to undertake a study of the related Isleteño. Therefore he sent me on ahead to Isleta Pueblo. When he broke free, he would go directly to Santa Fé, where I could join him later.

West of Chicago, on the open prairie, the train got a hot box (I never knew just what a hot box was, but trains were always getting them). There was, as always in such cases, a long delay and the passengers got out to stretch their legs by walking along the right-of-way.

I had forgotten how blue the sky could be, and how deep. It was like looking into a blue infinity. This was the sky of my childhood. The wind of my childhood blew across uncluttered miles, smelling fresh and wild, smelling of spring greenness. I did not precisely kneel down to kiss the western soil, but I stooped and picked a clover blossom and held it to my face.

VII Paisanos And Other Native Americans

IN THE FIRST year of our marriage, Harrington assigned me a piece of work to do on my own—not field-work, but copying the early baptismal records of Mission San Gabriel. He had been told that these records included the pagan name of the convert as well as the Christian name bestowed at baptism. In fact, I believe he had already had a look at them, but had not been able to spare the time to copy them himself. He secured permission for me to do this work, but did not go with me to the mission. I rang the bell in a state of nervous tension. Calling myself an atheist, I was not yet far removed from a strong Protestant background. Mystery and awe amounting almost to dread enveloped anything connected with Roman Catholicism. I know nothing of how I was supposed to conduct myself, and was almost afraid to speak for fear of making some outlandish error that would give offense.

A young priest conducted me to a very small room which I immediately characterized as a "cubicle." It accommodated a writing desk and a chair. I sat down, then the priest brought me several black-bound volumes whose yellow pages were almost crumbling with age. I think he said a word of caution on this account and I assured him I would take care. Probably because I had been told to ask for a certain person, I knew this young priest's name. Years afterward I began to see it mentioned in the newspapers at increasingly frequent intervals. He eventually became Bishop Buddy of the San Diego diocese.

I opened the ancient records with a reverence which turned to horror. They did indeed contain Indian proper names, but so carelessly written by persons who knew nothing of the language that they were of almost no linguistic value, especially since their meaning was not given in Spanish. What made chills run down my spine was the constantly reiterated notation that So-and-so, "neophyte of the Mission," was baptized *"in articulo mortis"* with "two soldiers of the guard" acting as sponsors. Showing my copy to Harrington, I asked him, "Did they club them and drag them in unconscious? Is that how the Church got its converts?"

Harrington's indignation was all for the cultures and languages which had been wiped out; I do not think he shared my almost overwhelming personal sense of participation in those long past agonies. I now began to realize something that I had scarcely thought of before: the suffering involved when a technologically superior culture, bent on conquest, impinges on native cultures which have been evolving at their own rate for millenia.

This was the prelude to my introduction to a distinct subculture which has doubtless ceased to exist, the descendants of its members having long since been absorbed into the mass of Spanish surnamed people who now choose to be known as "Chicanos." When I first listened to Harrington interviewing Spanish-speaking persons, I would ask, "Are they Indians or Mexicans." He soon put me straight. Very few of these people, he said, were Mexicans, and they did not care to be identified as Mexicans. They were descendants of soldiers or settlers who had come to California long before Mexico won its independence from Spain, and virtually all of them had some admixture of Indian blood, though not always tribally identifiable. They preferred to be known as *Californios* (Californians), or *paisanos,* country people, people who from time immemorial had lived upon this land. The *Californios* spoke a kind of Spanish which differed from the Spanish I had heard in Mexico. There were consonantal variations, of which I remember only that *Gabriel* was always *Graviel,* and *mucho, muncho.* Harrington always insisted that I write Spanish words exactly as I heard them, not as I thought they "ought to be" pronounced. The younger people tended to mix English words into their conversation. One sentence which Harrington was fond of quoting went like this: *"Fuimos al picnique y tuvimos muncho fon"* (We went to the picnic and had much fun).

This subculture had its social stratifications. I do not speak of the few aristocratic California families of pure Spanish descent, but of variations of status among the *paisanos.* There was a greatly respected couple who lived in a little narrow two-story adobe house at Calabasas (or could it have been Camarillo? I think Calabasas is correct). They were always addressed as "Don" and "Doña." I cannot remember their names. I hope they are to be found among the notes I left with Harrington, but I fear not, for in re-

cording my interviews with Doña Whatever-her-
name-was I always, as Harrington taught me, referred
to her by the impersonal "inf." for "informant."
Therefore, since it is awkward and confusing to be
continually writing "Don——" and "Doña——," I
shall refer to them in this narrative as "Don Juan"
and "Doña Marta"—but if either of these names hap-
pens to be correct, it is by sheer coincidence. Their
surname also escapes me, but it must have been
Basque, for Don Juan was descended from Basque
shepherds who came to California with Spanish settlers. Doña Marta was the last traceable descendant
of the tribe missionized at San Gabriel—the last
"Gravieleña." I have spoken of Anna, wife of Henry
whose ancestor was the Bear, as my first paid informant. Perhaps I should have assigned that position to
Doña Marta; but I never specifically paid her for information, only for food and lodging.

Harrington and I were together on our first visit to
the house at Calabasas; afterwards I always went
alone. On this first occasion they had other visitors,
two young couples to whom Don Juan gave sage advice. In comparison to these young people, Don Juan
and Doña Marta seemed very prosperous, very secure. For one couple they were providing a temporary
refuge. The husband had fallen afoul of the law and
was wanted for some serious crime—it may even have
been for murder, because I remember looking at his
thin, sad, gentle face and thinking that he did not look
like a murderer. This was my first encounter with
someone on the run from the law, and the problem of
guilt or innocence was uppermost in my mind. I asked
Doña Marta if she thought he had done what he was
accused of, and she answered, "Who knows?" She
said nothing else, but her whole demeanor implied,
What difference did it make: here was a fellow creature, one of her own kind, in need of succor—why
inquire what had brought him to this pass? These
pathetic youngsters did not come into the house except
for a few hurried, frightened moments. They occupied

an oblong wooden structure "out back," which I remember as resembling a very small freight car, although I don't think it really was. It had, at any rate, a wide wooden door where the couple sat side by side, feet dangling. The wife, pregnant of course, leaned against her husband, and both their faces were filled with woe. I believe there was some talk of their getting away to Mexico, but they seemed not to know how to go about it.

The other couple made themselves at home in the adobe. The husband consulted privately with Don Juan, while his wife chattered brashly. *"Vivimos en el Dompe"* (we live in the Dump), she announced with obvious pride. They had no means of transportation, so at the conclusion of our visit Harrington and I took them in the Ford to their home in the middle of the Los Angeles city dump, a shack made of scraps of board and flattened tin cans and God knows what.

On all my subsequent visits to the adobe at Calabasas, scattered at intervals over the remaining time that Harrington and I were together in California, I stayed overnight for at least one night. I became very familiar with the house and its environs. The front yard was a tangle of growth, including at least one fig tree, grape vines an a large *nopal* (clump of prickly pear). Behind the house was the rectangular shack, a chicken yard, a small cowbarn, and, back of all this, willows fringing a pool where the waters of a creek had accumulated. A fallen log stretched out over this pool. Here a black and white cat often crouched, ready to make swift paw-swipes at fish darting too close to the surface of the water.

The first of my overnight visits was probably in the late summer or early fall after our child was born—I know I was not pregnant at the time. After supper and a brief time spent in conversation, Doña Marta showed me up the steep and narrow stairs to the room which she occasionally rented to transients. She turned back the bedding, revealing sheets of coarse, unbleached cotton and proudly asked me to observe how clean they were. Only one person, she assured me, had slept in them since they had been washed, and he only for one night. This person was a cattle-drover from Los Angeles who always stayed with them when he passed that way: a fine man, very clean, very genteel. It took me some time to fall asleep. I couldn't help wondering what my mother would think if she knew that I was sleeping between sheets which had formerly enclosed the body of a genteel drover.

I do not believe Doña Marta knew many Indian words or was very sure of any that she may have remembered. Harrington must have considered her as a font of folklore and tradition which I could tap while he busied himself with more important subjects. I remember little of what she imparted to me; but something she said one evening as we sat alone together in the mellow glow of the kerosene lamp will remain with me as long as I live. Doña Marta had been speaking of her grandmother, who, she said, was a devout Catholic (*muy católica*) and an equally devout adherent of the Old Religion.

"How could that be?" I asked, convinced in my youthful absolutism that a person must either believe or disbelieve and could not possibly accept two different mythologies as equally valid statements of truth.

"My grandmother explained it this way," Doña Marta said. She held her hands in front of her, long, pale brown forefingers extended, and moved first one and then the other ahead. One could easily visualize two animals running neck and neck, alternating in the lead position. Doña Marta quoted her grandmother as saying, *"Los dos coren juntos* (the two run together). When one fails, the other helps."

Doña Marta said she herself had been "very wild" as a young girl. She had not listened to her grandmother's teaching, she had not cared to learn from anyone. Riding, shooting, running wild in the countryside had been her life. She also had played practical jokes with a streak of cruelty, or at least a disregard of others' sensibilities. Once, for example, she had shot a hawk, cooked it, and served it to her family, claiming that it was some other kind of fowl, then disgusting them later by revealing what they had eaten. Although she now appeared so disciplined and quiet, the element of unkindness still surfaced occasionally.

One Sunday she prepared an ample and delicious chicken dinner. After we had eaten, we two women lingered at the table while Don Juan stepped into the adjoining room and picked up a Spanish language newspaper. He was literate, though I don't believe Doña Marta could read at all.

Suddenly she burst out, "This man is nothing to me!"

I looked astonished and she elaborated, "This old man. My husband. I have never cared for him. He is nothing to me. Nothing!"

The rooms were small and the door stood open. Don Juan was actually only a few feet away. I was in an agony of apprehension lest he should overhear. Indeed, he could not help hearing the conversation, but he sat clamly, holding his paper before him; in all likelihood, it was not first time that he had heard these words.

I put my finger to my lips and indicated the open door. Doña Marta relentlessly continued to unfold her tale, not troubling to lower her voice. When she was very young, she said, she had been betrothed to a young man whom she loved with all her heart. But he had jilted her. Then, in spite, she had taken a solemn vow to marry the first man who came along. "And the first was this one—this old man, traveling with a pack on his back."

This story so exactly parelleled my own grandmother's that it gave me an eerie feeling. And my heart ached for poor Don Juan, who treated his wife with such unfailing consideration that I had pictured them as an ideal couple. I remembered how impressed I had been at our first meal together. Doña Marta placed a stack of tortillas on the table, wrapped in a clean white cloth to keep them warm and moist. Don

Juan seated her, then hastily opened the cloth and with a flourish laid the top (and therefore warmest and freshest) tortilla on his wife's plate. *"La primera es para ella"* (the first is for her), he said, *"siempre para ella"* (always for her).

Once when I planned to stay three or four days, Don Juan asked me if I would drive them to see friends in the Santa Monica mountains. These people, he gave me to understand, were very fine people indeed; they occupied a superior position among the *Californios* because they were the only surviving relatives of the *bandido,* Joaquín Murietta.

We set out early in the morning. Don Juan put a gallon jug in the car, explaining with a wink that he intended to bring it back full of *"agua del mar"* (sea water). Dismayed, I tried to explain in my halting Spanish that the Ford was not in good enough condition to make the hard climb up from the coast. *"La máquina no anda bien"* (the machine doesn't go well), I said. Don Juan, blithely disregarding my remarks, seated his wife in the back and took his place beside me so that he could give directions.

High up in the mountains, on a road walled in on both sides by scrub oak and chamizo thickets, he warned me to proceed slowly, *despacito*—I really couldn't go any other way, considering the gradient and the condition of the car—while he watched for the proper turnoff. Soon he directed me onto a track, actually two parallel ruts, angling off into the undergrowth. Bumping and struggling along this winding way, we emerged suddenly into a roughly circular clearing fringed with pink and white oleanders. These oleander bushes appeared to be quite old; their trunks were large and they were as tall as the wild growth behind them. Don Juan told me to stop. He got out and walked toward a weathered, unpainted frame house, calling out to announce his presence. An old man crossed the clearing and greeted him enthusiastically. Then a woman appeared at the door. Doña Marta and I were invited to come into the house, and

Don Juan introduced me as a friend who owned a *máquina*.

Inside the house we found a woman in late middle age, presumably the wife of the gentleman who had welcomed us, and four or five younger women. Doña Marta was very much at home. I could not follow all the exchanges in rapid Spanish, but at times I was courteously included in the conversation. On the wall hung an enlarged photograph, crudely hand-colored in pastels, of a young woman. She, I was informed, was very intelligent, very highly educated, and held a sec-retarial position in Los Angeles. Second only to the notable Joaquin, this young woman was highly es-teemed as having enhanced the family's standing. I do not remember—if I heard—what the family surname was. I gathered that relationship to the illustrious bandit was on the mother's side, but in this I could have been mistaken.

An enormous meal was in preparation on the wood-burning range. There was a large pot of chicken stew-ing in rich sauce and an even larger pot from which beans were ladled into iron skillets for refrying. A young woman was patting out tortillas and deftly flip-ping them from one side to the other to brown lightly on top of the stove. A few steps from the front door long boards were laid across sawhorses, and this trestle was flanked by crude, backless wooden benches. When the food was ready and the coffee boiling, ta-blecloths were spread and places set. It seemed to me pleasant that we were to eat outdoors picnic fashion, though I wondered a little that there were so many more places than people.

Our host sat at the farthest end of the table, Don Juan at the end nearest the house, and I was seated on Don Juan's left. Then iron clanged on iron and al-most at once, from the whole perimeter of the clear-ing, young men came out, ten or a dozen grim, swarthy youths with close-cropped bullet heads. In silence, they approached the table; in silence, they sat down. If they acknowledged Don Juan's presence, it was briefly and without change of expression. Me they ignored. These must have been husbands, brothers, or cousins of the young women in the house, yet when a woman came out with fresh coffee or tortillas, no pleasantries were exchanged. A jug of wine passed from hand to hand, and they drank as they had eaten in ominous silence. Don Juan and his friend did not attempt conversation down the length of that silent table. I, too, ate in silence, eyes fixed on my plate, less in timidity than in sheer terror. When the young men had finished, they rose as one and silently melted into the oleanders, like ghosts disappearing into a wall. But these youths were not in the least ephemeral: they were as solid, as uncompromisingly menacing, as loaded weapons, although they had doubtless come to the table from quite innocent work in hidden strips of field or vineyard. I have tried to tell myself that they were probably quite harmless persons, as exemplary in their way as their female relative who was a secretary in Los Angeles. To this day I do not believe it. These were scions of a family in which banditry was the most honorable profession. I cannot think that their aura of potential violence was entirely the product of my over-active imagination. They move through my memory like the disciplined nucleus of a guerrilla army.

Left alone, Don Juan and the gentleman of the house resumed their placid, leisurely banter. Women came out and cleared the table. Don Juan went to the car and fetched his jug. He carried it with him into the oleanders, presently to emerge, winking and smiling, telling me that he had his "sea water" (by which I belatedly understood he meant wine) and now we were ready to go home.

All my visits to the house at Calabasas were enriching experiences. At the time, even as I enjoyed them, I also felt resentful. Each one meant curtailing or omitting a visit to my family. I wish I could recall what precisely was the line of enquiry that made them so important; certainly it was not linguistic, else Harrington would have been on the spot. As it was, I do not think he saw Don Juan and Doña Marta after the day he introduced me to them. These visits were, of course, only brief and rather charming interludes. Perhaps Harrington regarded them as training for me, but I do not think he reasoned it that way.

When I was with Harrington in the field, in addition to my ordinary task as cook, chauffeur, and typist, I was, as I have said, learning to be a rather half-hearted linguist and an enthusiastic gatherer of myths, whenever I could find a not too reluctant informant. However, it was the work I did in that wretched combination kitchen and dining room in Washington which convinced him that he could send me out on my own. My work on the Taos language included other facets besides the pronoun. Somewhere among my manuscripts is a black notebook labeled "Taos Grammar." I must have compiled it myself, for I left with Harrington everything that was his and much that, strictly speaking, was not.

Even though I was well prepared linguistically, I was still dreadfully shy of strange people. I approached Isleta Pueblo literally in fear and trembling. My composure was further shaken by an episode on the train shortly before it reached Albuquerque. In a stout cloth bag, pinned by a large safety pin to my "corset-cover" (which was what we called the ancestress of the bra), I carried three hundred dollars. Dressing in my berth early in the morning, I could not find this essential garment. I shook out all my clothing piece by piece, I explored every fold of sheets and blankets, I looked over the edge of the berth behind the curtains. Nothing! I was in despair. There was very little in my purse, not enough for food and a hotel room. I thought desperately of writing my people—but where would I wait while they sent money for my rescue? And if they sent me money, I would be obligated to go straight home instead of doing the work that had been assigned to me. I thought of the terrible things that would be said about my carelessness, not only by Harrington but by my own parents as well. I was still young, relatively inexperienced—and at the moment very frightened. Finally, I decided the first step would be to summon the conductor. I slipped on my dress and parted the curtains of the berth. There in the middle of the narrow aisle lay the missing garment. I reached out a shaking arm and retrieved it. Judging by its appearance, it had lain in the aisle all night and had been trodden on several times. But the money was intact.

When I try to remember Isleta, there is again a strange duality. It seems that I must have stayed there twice, yet I am virtually sure that it was only once. Perhaps this comes from my having done two types of work there: one which I can take pride in to this day and another of which I felt ashamed even as I did it. Or it may be because I clearly picture two white families, one decent and respectable, the other living in squalor.

The latter consisted of the Indian Agent, his wife, and children. I went to them when I first reached the pueblo to see about securing a place to live and an informant. They were from somewhere in the South, the kind of people that my mother described as "poor white trash." The man, presumably, was to advise the men of the pueblo, whose ancestors had farmed for centuries, on agricultural methods—and heaven help the women if they were supposed to take his wife as a model in domestic matters! On first entering their house, I was struck by the stench. Then something hissed at me from behind a door. It proved to be a pet owl, which emerged dragging rabbit entrails across the bare floor. The loutish boys of the household shot rabbits for it daily, and it ate them wherever it pleased. Another source of odor was the bathtub, in which piles of dirty overalls soaked for days on end. The weather was hot, and a green scum formed over the stale, soapy water. The Agent's wife was large and slovenly, and held all Indians in contempt.

I think the head of the other white family had something to do with the railroad. Theirs was a neat and wholesome household. They kept white rabbits in cages, and the youngest girl had them all named and cried at the thought of eating them. I had Sunday dinner with them once—fried rabbit. They were kindly people, but disinterested in Indians. Not prejudiced, not contemptuous, merely disinterested.

There were in the pueblo, apart from the communal dwellings, several small detached houses. I was permitted to live in a rather isolated one-room adobe, whitewashed outside (as were all the other buildings), cool and dim inside, with a hard-packed dirt floor.

Daytime in Isleta I was not at all lonely. There was much to do and I was eager to prove myself. But at night, walking in moonlight on white sands, looking longingly at the ghostly white pueblo where people lived with each other, my heart ached with emptiness. This was not the frightened desperate loneliness I had experienced on the Tejon Ranch. It was an adult, more poignant variety of that loneliness I felt when, aged thirteen, I sat on the front steps of my parents' home, drenched in the fragrance of lilacs, listening to the distant sound of a violin coming from a hall downtown, where people were dancing, and wondering if I would ever go to a dance or ever have a lover. But the undefined figure of the beloved who would fulfill my life did not now bear the slightest resemblance to Harrington. I wrote to him several times a week, reporting what I felt was very good progress with the language of Isleta, and there were certain linguistic matters I would have liked to discuss with him—aside from which, I had no desire for his presence.

My first informant was a pretty, gentle young woman named Felicitas. She wore the dress of the pueblo: black woolen garment fastened over one shoulder and worn over a blouse or shift, white buckskin moccasins with leg wrappings extending to just below the knee. Well-to-do women had very thick leg wrappings and many strings of beads. Felícitas was very poor, the sole support of a four-year-old boy.

The shape of her calves was not hidden by bulky wrappings, and she had only one string of beads. Her child's name was Alejandro. He was constantly disappearing and she was constantly calling him: "Alejandruuu! Alejandruuu!" One of his favorite tricks was to lie completely immobile perilously close to the railroad tracks. Whenever I recall June in Isleta, I see a willful little boy and a lizard with a bright blue tail, both half-buried in whitish dust.

In addition to teaching me Isleteño, Felícitas, gently reproving my disorderliness, kept my papers, pots, and pans neatly put away and my floor hardpacked and dust free. She appeared to enjoy working and talking with me, although my Spanish was not fluent and she had very little English. What she did not enjoy was working once a week for the wife of the Indian Agent. The filth revolted her, the children made sport of her and teased Alejandro, and, most humiliating of all, after the family had eaten, the sluttish woman would empty a child's plate of leftovers, wipe it off with a piece of bread, and slap some food on it for Felícitas —who would then work fasting all day rather than eat from an unwashed plate.

I liked working with a cooperative informant, fluent in her own language. It soon became apparent that of the two languages the one spoken in Taos was older, nearer to the mother tongue. The people of Isleta tended to speak more rapidly and to bite off their words. The only word I remember in both languages was the work for "sizzling" (as meat sizzles over a fire). In Taos, they said *tisililima* (1 representing what Harrington called the "Welsh l," that is, a sound produced with the sides of the tongue touching the palate, and the last vowel strongly nasal). In Isleta, it became *tsiriri'im*, lips closing firmly after the m. Structurally the languages were much alike—perhaps the Isleta pronoun was somewhat less complex, after all these years I'm really not sure.

My other informant was Luis Abeita. A member of an influential pueblo family, he had now been em-

ployed for some years as Indian policeman. I think it
may have been the long association with whites,
forced on him by this job, which made him willing to
work for me. He could use the extra money for his
growing family, but that might not have been sufficient
for most men of the pueblo; although, of course, it
was Felícitas' impoverishment which forced her to
work for the family of the Indian Agent and also for
me.

On the surface presenting a more open society than
that of Taos, the people of Isleta were in their own
way quite as conservative, quite as unwilling to open
their life style and sacred beliefs to the eyes and
thought of aliens. At this time, however, the relationship in Isleta Pueblo between Roman Catholicism and
the Old Religion resembled that happy cooperation
described by Doña Marta's grandmother: "the two
ran together." A man would do his stint on the church
(one day's work per month, if I am not mistaken) and
attend night-long ceremonies in the kiva, and no one
objected or thought it strange. Church bells and chants
did not conflict with ancient songs and ritual dances.
But I recently read (in *The Death of God,* by Earl
Shorris) that a too-zealous monsignor changed all that
and now the church is closed.

Luis Abeita was small, like most pueblo men, but
strong, mentally and physically. The demands of his
work had hardened him and made him slightly cynical. He was very protective of his wife and children.
When he complained about having to leave them behind on his frequent trips to Gallup, New Mexico, I
asked why he didn't take them along sometimes.
Never, he replied, that town was "too tough."

Harrington was pleased with what I was getting on
the Isleta language, but he now began bombarding me
with demands to "get something on kachinas to satisfy
Fewkes." It seems Doctor Fewkes had made a polite
and casual inquiry as to whether he knew anything
about the kachinas of Isleta Pueblo, and Harrington
had taken this as a directive which must be obeyed.

My time in Isleta was growing short, and I was told I must do something quickly.

Now comes the episode of which, I am heartily ashamed. I laid the kachina problem before my informant. He dodged it, saying that his work as policeman had cut him off from those who practised the old ways. But surely, I persisted, he had seen the kachinas? Yes, he admitted reluctantly, as a boy he had seen them; but he really didn't remember. Surely he remembered something. Maybe. If I showed him pictures of kachinas would he point out those that looked like the Isleta kachinas? Would he try to draw them?

Tongue in cheek, he agreed. I furnished pictures, paper, and crayons, and he selected a few kachinas, gave them Isleteño names, and proceeded to draw them, with certain variations. Suddenly he seized the green crayon and began to draw a kachina like nothing in the pictures. He gave it a name. When I excitedly asked him about it, he said he had made it up.

Never before or since have I done anything professionally that was not meticulously honest. The matter haunted me for years, but failed to trouble Harrington—although in his linguistic work he would hear a word many times in order to record it with great precision. He showed the drawings I sent him to Dr. Fewkes, whose only comment was "interesting." I was so bitterly ashamed of the whole transaction that I ended up by not letting myself think of it. Now reviewing it in proper perspective, I doubt that my informant was as alienated, let alone as ignorant, as he pretended to be; and I think that at least in the predominantly green kachina we may have had something approximating an authentic Kachina of Isleta. In short, I think Mr. Abeita was putting me on.

Eventually Harrington arrived in Santa Fé, and we stayed there or in Taos Village for some time. I don't remember travelling back to California with him, and I assume that he again sent me on alone. In fact, it must have been on my way home that I stopped over for a day at Zuñi Pueblo. Harrington had heard that Kroeber was interested in the Zuñi, and therefore he wanted me to get a sample of the language.

I was directed to a young man who was said to be a graduate of Carlisle. What a relief, I thought, to be able to work with someone who spoke both his own language and English! My rejoicing was ill-timed. This man was the slowest speaking person I ever encountered, with the sole exception of the Kiowas we spoke with in Washington. I don't think I had more than a page of notes to show for a whole day's work.

The Zuñi informant's last name was Shattuck and my mother's maiden name was Chaddock. This similarity caused me to mention him to her when I at last reached home for a visit, in what must have been late summer or early autumn.

"He's your cousin," she at once declared. She explained that one of her older brothers had left a cattle drive somewhere in New Mexico "to go with the Indians," and that this man was undoubtedly his son or grandson.

I wanted to know whereabouts in New Mexico my uncle had left the drive and what tribe he had joined, and I reminded my mother that the name was spelled differently. She brushed aside all objections.

"Makes no difference," she insisted with a finalizing sniff. "He's your cousin."

VIII An End To Idolatry

THE AREA IN the San Bernardino Mountains of Southern California around Big Bear and Lake Arrowhead tantalized Harrington. A number of his informants claimed to know something about it. They had been there in their youth, or their parents or grandparents had roamed over that country. Yet for a long time we could get no one to accompany us on a trip through that region. We made two or three preliminary trips by ourselves, trying to locate places which had been named and roughly described. The road presented no

119

such difficulties as the one leading up towards the head-waters of the Tule River, but it was still, at that time, narrow and unpaved with many steep pitches; indubitably a mountain road. During one descent, the brakeband burned out. That was more or less routine on the Model T—when it happened, you simply used the reverse pedal to slow you up or the low gear. But when all the bands were gone, you had to drag along at the side of the road. Once we came down in that fashion to the level country without enough braking ability to slow down for a street crossing.

Ultimately, after our return from New Mexico, Harrington located an informant who claimed he knew the San Bernardino mountains and was willing to go with us. This as it turned out was the last trip we were to take in the mountains, actually our last field trip together that I recall in any detail. Parts of this expedition have proved unforgettable. I can even date it: November, 1918. The shadow of Prohibition lay heavy across the land, and saloons below Main Street in Los Angeles were selling off their stocks at bargain prices. The scene was bedlam—drunks rushing in to buy bottles, drinking up the contents and elbowing their way back to buy more, for as long as the money lasted or as long as they could keep their feet, because for them there was no tomorrow. One of the conditions Manuel, the informant, had laid down was that he should be furnished liquor on this trip. He was a sturdy man in his late fifties or early sixties, powerfully built and stubborn of disposition. We picked him up in the vicinity of Highland and drove back to Los Angeles, where he became insistent on the subject of booze. Harrington said it would be most inappropriate and even dangerous for a man in his position to buy liquor for an Indian. Accordingly, he had me stop the car a block or so away on the opposite side of the street, and sent me into the mad-house of a skidrow saloon to purchase two bottles of cheap whiskey. At that time, women, at least middle-class women brought up as I had been, simply did not enter saloons. For the brief time it lasted, it was a humiliating experience. Drunks shoved against me, leered, or shouted at me. But I made my way to the bar and came out with the whiskey in a brown paper bag. Then we started for the mountains.

I'm vague about where we stayed the first night. It was indoors and there is an impression of one or two other people, so it might have been at a camp not quite closed for the winter. But I'm sure Harrington didn't pay anything. I remember going outdoors alone shortly before we ate. The night was dark and crisply cold. There was still a bottle of whiskey left. I broke off some lettuce leaves (on this expedition I had resolved that we should eat better than usual and had bought a few vegetables to take along), and gnawed a bit of jerky, washing the snack down with a swallow of Manuel's whiskey, very warming to the insides. This and the mountain air made me feel unusually good. On my visit home, I had purchased a warm sweater and a pair of sturdy, high-laced shoes, almost like boots, so I was comfortably dressed. Everything contributed to a sense of happy adventure I had not felt for a long time.

The next morning we drove leisurely on in bright sunlight, stopping now and then for Harrington and the informant to explore on foot. Snow had not yet entirely covered the ground and the road was clear. We passed a resort store that was still open. Manuel demanded beer. All they had was a near-beer called Bevo, but Manuel was not literate. Harrington bought him several bottles, and, not realizing that it was non-alcoholic, Manuel experienced all the desired effects. To put it plainly, he got quite satisfactorily drunk. That was a bit of fun that Harrington and I could share.

A few evenings later everything had changed. Snow had fallen intermittently all day, and at this elevation it had already been lying on the ground for sometime. Manuel sat huddled in a blanket. He demanded shelter and there was none to be had. Very late in the afternoon we came to a resort already closed for the winter. The accommodations provided for summer campers consisted of boarded boxlike bases, doorless and open to one side, with canvass tops. Now most of the canvass had been taken down or blown away, so these tent-houses did not offer much in the way of protection from the weather. There was one well-built, comfortable-looking house with the blessed signal of smoke issuing from the chimney. Manuel was emphatic about wanting to stay in the house. Harrington said he would do his best.

A man came to the door and quite a long colloquy ensued. Once I heard the plaintive words, "But I've got this old Indian with me." The man said "No" firmly, gestured toward what remained of the tent camp, closed the door.

Harrington came back to tell us dejectedly, "He won't take us in the house. He says we can sleep in that tent-house that still has some canvass on it."

The sun had now set. Dusk was falling rapidly. I was colder than I had ever been in my life, and for some reason—I attributed it to the intense cold—every breath was painful. There was a stove, partially exposed and with the firebox drifted part way full of snow. I cleaned it out as best I could with my hands, but a layer of ice remained at the bottom. There was a stack of stovelength logs, also snow encrusted. I got newspaper from the car to try, almost without hope, to start a fire. Manuel dragged himself up, coughing a little, brought me a handful of twigs, then returned to his blanket. I brought out the big battered aluminum pot and the iron skillet. I got out food, the head of cauliflower, and the big cheap steaks that I had bought in the lowlands and had looked forward to preparing in a pleasant, picnic environment. Everything was frozen solid. The newspaper took fire, Manuel's twigs blazed briefly, but the logs showed no sign of igniting. All that I did now was lethargic, slow-motion, paralyzed by the merciless, bone-shattering cold.

The man in the house must have been observing us from a window. I heard his call to Harrington, "Hey, you! Come here." Harrington complied, and the man exclaimed, "God Almighty, why didn't you tell me you had a woman with you?"

Harrington came back to our forlorn campsite and told us the man had changed his mind. Missing the point, he grumbled to me, "But I *told* him I had this old Indian with me."

He hustled Manuel out of the cold, and I trailed after. The man had two large frying-pans full of something, what I don't remember, and he said there was enough for all, no need for me to cook. Fire blazed in the fireplace, the stove glowed, the room and the food were warm, but my deepseated shivering would not abate. After we ate I drew my chair close to the fire and stretched out my feet to the flames. Harrington spoke to me sharply. He said heat would ruin the leather, wet shoes should be dried slowly, on the feet.

Manual brought in his bedding, warmed it briefly and went to the place assigned to him. Harrington felt we owed a debt of gratitude to our host. It was his duty now to chat with the man, entertain him, create a good impression.

The owner of the camp said that in another week he would have been gone. After the rush of the tourist season, he liked a little time alone with his dogs before he went down to the coast. The dogs were big, beautiful, intelligent. Their master set the skillets down for them to clean out. This shocked and charmed me. My finicky mother had never permitted an animal to eat from a vessel in which human food was prepared. For a time, I listened to the talk and watched the dogs. Then I asked Harrington to spread out our bedroll by the fire so that the blankets would have a chance to dry and get warm through. He brushed me off. Later, still cold and now almost light-headed with fatigue, I repeated my request. He shushed me as one would an importunate child. Our host looked from one to the other of us curiously, but did not interfere. I think he may finally have given a hint about having to get up in the morning.

At any rate, the seemingly endless evening did come to an end, and Harrington got our roll of bedding and carried it into the unheated room where we were to sleep. Snow had sifted into one end of the roll. As it melted, the blankets were permeated with a damp chill, and I seemed unable to generate any body warmth. My feet were so icy that Harrington asked me not to touch him.

By morning I was warm enough, but felt too sick to eat breakfast. All day my fever mounted, and I fought the snowy roads in a daze that was half delirium. Manuel was coughing incessantly. Mercifully, sometime in the afternoon we reached a resort that was still partially open. Even Harrington could see that I was too ill to camp out, and he was concerned about Manuel. He rented two rooms. In the evening he went out to get something to eat. He was gone rather a long time and came back highly excited. The news had just come in: the armistice was signed and the war over. It will be remembered that another event besides the end of the war marked this period. The country had its first epidemic of what we then called "Spanish influenza." Manuel and I were among the early cases. Later people in the cities went about wearing gauze masks for fear of contagion.

That night I lay in a strange room, in the unaccustomed comfort of a bed, trying to breathe, alternately falling in and out of nightmares and staring up at the open beams of the ceiling, which had been draped with pine branches. In the dim, uncertain light these branches looked to me like dismembered corpses. I knew they weren't. I knew that was a delusion, but when I closed my eyes—or sometimes with them open—my mind supplied gruesome details.

In the morning, Harrington went to see how Manuel was doing, intending to buy him a good breakfast and "jolly him up." Manuel was gone. He had risen at first light, inquired about the possibility of getting a ride to Los Angeles, and set off on foot across the snowy mountains. I hope he made it. If he didn't, I hope he at least made it home to die. Indians are peculiarly susceptible to respiratory diseases.

We may have stayed at the lodge two nights, certainly not longer, perhaps only one night and half the next morning. Harrington decided I was well enough to drive and that we would finish the trip as planned, though unfortunately without our informant. This plan called for descending the steep, tortuous road down the inland slope of the mountain range. My fever was down somewhat, but I was very weak. I really do not know how I ever got that Ford down to the high desert. Consciousness was a tight circle maintained by will alone; in its dark ambience, hallucinations wavered. Half the time I didn't quite know which was the real road and which the dream, and my erratic driving elicited several sharp yelps from my companion. But, oh, how well I remember the blessed relief of reaching the foot of the mountain! My mind seemed to clear at once. There was a sort of town there, almost like a ghost town. I recall an unpainted building with a false front, gray with age, which housed a general store. And I remember cottonwoods, still green, and moving in a mild, dry wind, a healing wind that immediately began to penetrate my clogged bronchial tubes.

I told Harrington no, I didn't want any mush, but I could drink some tomato soup. He bought a can of Campbells' tomato soup at the store and volunteered to fix it for me, which he did, by dumping it into a very large pot of hot water. I peevishly refused to drink more than one cupful of the thin, nauseous beverage. Harrington was hurt. He felt I was both ungrateful and unreasonable. After all, the only reason the direction said to add one cup of water to one can of soup was so that they could sell more.

The next day we drove on into the Mohave Desert on the route we would have taken had Manuel remained with us. I am sure we went as far as Barstow, perhaps farther, and we must have camped out several nights. The only details that are distinct in memory concern the dragonflies. We reached an area where there had been a heavy downpour. The sun shown brightly on pools of rainwater and around and above every one of them hovered swarms of dragonflies. Heretofore, I had thought of a dragonfly as a smallish insect. Some were gold, some bright metallic green, others scarlet. I could not believe they were real, I could not get enough of watching them. They had even more of the quality of other-worldliness than the newt that had enthralled me by the streambed near Santa Ynez in a time not actually long past, though in retrospect it seemed like something experienced by a different person in a vanished age. In another period of my life, I would come to think of the dragonfly as a shaman's scout, a messenger or intermediary between the human world and the mysterious world of animal familiars. That was a bit of esoteric knowledge I had yet to learn.

I can't say how long we drove about in the desert, nor what the object of our trip was, nor anything that we talked about (except the dragonflies), nor if Harrington searched for and found an informant. Eventually I must have taken Harrington back to his base at the Southwest Museum and have gone on myself to San Diego, for I have the impression that I rested there till I stopped spitting blood. I saw city-dwellers wearing their "flu masks" and came to understand that many persons far better cared for than I had succumbed. Logic dictates that I remained till after Christmas. I don't know. All Christmases at home are merged into one.

The rest of the winter and early spring is a meaningless, directionless jumble of skidding about in heavy rain, grateful when we were able to stay in the ruts and thus avoid going off the road and getting completely mired down. Of course, since this was California, the sun did come out occasionally and when it did, it was sometimes bright and warm. On such a day as we proceeded in a sort of convoy of three or four cars laboring along through the mud, we caught up with a pair of Japanese youths, presumably students.

Their little car was not of standard width, so the ruts were of no benefit to them. Moreover, they were lost and nobody seemed able to understand their courteous questions. They wanted to know, "Which way Wa-warupe?" which Harrington at once interpreted as meaning, "What is the way to Guadalupe Mission?" This encounter led, as we struggled on our way, to an erudite discourse on the Japanese language, particularly its phonetic components.

It must have been during this season that I paid my last visit to Don Juan and Doña Marta, for I remember the dampness and the early dark. It was my custom always to pay for their hospitality with a bright gold coin, five or ten dollars according to the length of my stay, discreetly put in Doña Marta's hand at the time of parting. This time, for some reason, I gave it to her when I first arrived, and was immediately asked to drive them to town for supplies. They bought, I noticed, only staples: beans and flour, coffee, and a little sugar, with a smallish slice of California jack cheese as the only luxury.

Preparing supper by lamplight, crumbling the pale cheese sparingly over beans she had been refrying, Doña Marta confessed almost emotionally that I had helped them very much by coming at this time. She kept her voice low, so that Don Juan, sitting in the dining room, would not overhear. She had had no compunction about his overhearing her story of a loveless marriage, but she would not shame him by admitting to poverty in his hearing. (Which makes me wonder if both of them had not known all along that her claim of his meaning nothing to her was more fantasy than fact.)

Previously, Don Juan had gone out to milk the cow before breakfast and before supper. Then Doña Marta had poured the still warm milk into a large open pan, placed it on top of the stove and stirred it while it came to a boil. Both she and Don Juan considered milk unwholesome, almost deadly, unless it had been boiled.

Now Don Juan sat quietly in the house and there was no milk in sight. Had the cow gone dry? I asked.

The cow "*se mamaba solo*" (sucked her own milk), she replied, and they had had to sell her. I had known ever since I began to visit them of this problem with the cow, because of the forked stick fastened like a yoke around her neck; now I surmised that they had sold her, not because of her bad habit, but to get a little desperately needed cash.

The bright patina of security and modestly comfortable living had vanished with the mellow glow of summer. Here were an old man and an aging woman living in dire poverty, uncertain of their future, a picture stripped of all its glamor. It had never occurred to me before to ask myself what they lived on. Don Juan did not, to my knowledge, go out to work, though that is not to say he may not have done an occasional odd job. Perhaps he was a sort of benevolent *brujo*, and the young men who came to consult him paid for his services—but at best they could have paid only a pittance. The bedroom which they rented so proudly must have been infrequently occupied. Social security and welfare had not yet entered upon the scene. Did the crumbling adobe actually belong to them (if so, there must have been taxes), or did they merely live there by sufferance? These questions were never answered, for I never saw them again.

I do not know if any plan governed Harrington's peregrinations up and down and across southern and central California. I am inclined to think not. The vessel of the old culture was broken and the precious contents were flowing away and evaporating before our very eyes. Harrington lapped like a man dying of thirst at every random trickle. He rushed here and there, tracking down rumors of possible informants, and when he did find someone who even partially remembered the language of a vanished or vanishing people, he spent much more time with him than he had intended to spend with one informant and reproached himself afterwards for the delay. All that he learned became his own private treasure, something he felt he could not quite yet bring himself to share by publication, something that would always require a little more work, a little further exploration. Naturally this attitude carried over to information acquired about other languages which were not at the moment on the point of becoming extinct. I know that in time Harrington published, for I have seen him quoted in the writings of Levi-Strauss and others, but his publications surely constitute the merest fragment of the wealth of material he accumulated.

However the cold months of 1918-19 were spent, spring found us once more at Santa Ynez. Or was it Santa Ynez? In memory, the green hills look like the hills around that town. Or perhaps I only envision it as Santa Ynez because it seems fitting that the beginning of the end should have the same locale as the end of the beginning. Wherever we were, the marvelous typewriter had at last been delivered. It was a monstrously heavy machine, almost beyond my capacity to lift even in the strength of youth. But it had every letter, every symbol that Harrington desired. I was as excited about it as he, willingly stretching the weak and somewhat ineffective little finger of each hand to cover two more rows of keys, heroically determined to employ the touch system even on this giant. It was a time of comparative harmony and shared enthusiasms.

Also it was a time that Harrington chose to interrupt by talking about my taking another field trip alone. He said that he was going to stave off the return to Washington as long as possible, but when he got back he would surely have to publish. To this end, he thought it would be better for him to spend the summer filling the gaps in his Tanoan material. But he saw no reason why my time should be wasted. He needed a complete vocabulary and something on the structure of a language definitely recognized as Uto-Aztecan; therefore, he proposed sending me to a place where Paiute was spoken.

My objection was that I wanted to spend most of the summer at home, getting reacquainted with my children. Afterwards, I would like to join him in New Mexico, which I enjoyed. I still shrank from going alone into a totally strange place, and no longer felt it necessary to save face by pretending that I didn't. One of the cliches I had used in defending my roving existence to my mother was that a wife's place was with her husband, but now it seemed that more and more often my place was out in the field alone—which I would have accepted readily enough if I could have been truly independent, if I could have held in my own right a position comparable to Harrington's.

After I had resisted his arguments for sometime, Harrington offered to let me take my family with me. I don't know just where he first intended to send me. The picture he painted included plentiful informants, a salubrious climate, and mountain scenery that would be sure to appeal to my mother. It sounded enticing. I wrote home and Mother, always eager for new sights, consented to the project.

Almost on the eve of my departure for San Diego, Harrington changed his mind. The Chemehuevis, he said, spoke a Uto-Aztecan language and it was more nearly extinct than the Paiute. I would, therefore, take myself and my family to Parker, Arizona, there to gather all that I possibly could on the Chemehuevi. I don't know what influenced this decision. Probably Sapir's (?) secretly scanned paper had a share in it, and it is possible that Manuel, who walked away from us into the snow, may have been a Chemehuevi residing at Highland.

Harrington himself had told me about the Parker climate. Sometime, I don't know just when, but it was before we met, he had been there or in the vicinity working with a Mohave informant. (That was when he gathered material on Mohave beliefs about life after death, later incorporated in his lecture given at the Temple of Isis.) An incident of this trip which he frequently recounted concerned himself and another student lying on their blankets early in the morning, pretending to be asleep, while watching an Indian woman get dressed and counting the number of skirts she put on. He considered this a very funny story, a matter of scientific observation without lascivious intent. When he told it, mention of the intense heat and the bugs was generally included.

Too much heat made me ill, and Harrington knew it. Also my mother could not stand heat very well. It seemed an invitation to disaster to attempt to drag her and two small children into the God-forsaken and insect-ridden environment he had previously described. Now, of course his emphasis had shifted to the importance of the Chemehuevi language, and the place where he wanted me to go really wasn't too bad.

The altercation raged day and night. It was the story of our bitter quarrel about which make of car to purchase all over again—only now I was no longer desolate at the thought of disagreeing with my husband, and probably gave as good as I got. However, I inevitably gave in. I wrote my mother of the change of plan, and she reluctantly agreed to it. An unpleasant trip was better than no trip at all; besides, it was her duty to facilitate my being with the children. There was no question of trying to drive the Ford. After the fewest possible days of preparation at home we would take the train—in those days, passenger trains still ran to Parker. It was all Harrington's decision; I was sullen, rebellious, totally lacking in enthusiasm, although in my letters to my mother I pretended enthusiasm in order to keep her from backing out.

The day came for me to start home. We had been awake almost all night, prolonging the futile argument, and I felt completely drained. Harrington got into the car with me. When I looked at him in surprise, he said, "I'll ride out to the edge of town with you." This was an unexpected gesture. Two years before it would have thrilled me; now it left me cold.

We drove out of sight of the houses. Harrington told me to stop, this was far enough for him to walk back.

The green of April, April after a rainy winter, was all around. Dutifully he took me in his arms. I was passive. The stale smell of his clothing was offensive. Something—perhaps my lack of response to his show of affection—caused that now-familiar scowl which I had first seen when he entered the classroom in San Diego to flit across his face. I did not say anything out loud, except possibly "Good-bye;" but in my mind the response was distinctly articulated.

."I called him an angry god," I thought in amazement, "and all the while he was just a dirty little boy having a tantrum."

Harrington got out. I drove off and left him standing there. I am sure he was standing, looking after me, although it would have been more in character for him to have been striding rapidly away, his mind already fixed on linguistic problems. Before I saw him again, I would have experienced that moment of alchemic transformation, that "meeting of the eyes" which committed me to another man for life—and for eternity, if there should happen to be such a thing as an enduring soul.

In San Diego, I found that the baby was now talking. Less fluent than her precocious half-sister had been at slightly past two, she was nonetheless learning rapidly. Harrington had insisted that she be taught to call me *stau,* the Chumash word for "mother." (To the best of my recollection, this is the only stipulation he ever made as to her upbringing and education.) The child pronounced the word *shlau,* which was near enough. She liked the sound of it and was pleasurably excited at having another member of the household to admire her. Trotting at my heels, she piped incessantly, "Shlau, shlau, shlau." But for any real mothering, she turned to her grandmother.

This trip, like the one to the Tejon Ranch, began auspiciously. The train passed through Carrizo Gorge. My mother marvelled at the wild desert scenery, the children were happy and excited. But they were thoroughly tired by the time we got off at Parker.

The whistle sounded, the train chugged away into blackness. The dark was absolute. It was what I used to picture as a little child when my mother would describe "Egyptian darkness" to me as we lay in bed together on a summer night. Here in Parker (as possibly in Egypt!), a hot wind was blowing, carrying sand that blotted out the stars, abraded the skin, and inflamed the eyes. Our suitcases and other impedimenta of travel piled at our feet, my mother and I stood where we had got off, each holding a whimpering sleepy child. The only visible light was the dim glow of a lantern, far down at the other end of the station platform.

My mother described the situation succinctly. "This," she said, "is the jumping-off place."

Eventually we found someone, or someone found us and we were guided to the hotel. Our room was airless, gritty, and hot. A single fly-specked electric light bulb hung by a cord from the ceiling. There was a rickety iron double bed which had been painted white and now was dingy from grime and wear, and a few other meager furnishings. We still, according to my mother, were at "the jumping-off place."

In the morning, I saw the Indian Agent (who turned out to be a cut above his opposite number at Isleta) and a few other people, and we moved to a couple of rooms in a house on the reservation, then known as the Colorado River Indian Reservation. This house fronted on alfalfa fields. The air was filled with the green scent of freshly cut fields mingled with the wilder aromas of the encompassing desert. In spite of screens, flies were bad in the daytime; but bats kept mosquitoes and other flying insects in check, swooping and darting over the fields at dusk with shrill cries, almost out of the range of human ears, but doubtless loud and exciting to themselves.

The house was high off the ground. In the evening, I reached my hand out in the soft earth underneath it and collected toads, putting them in a cardboard box for the delectation of the children. Their grandmother warned them not to touch the toads, asserting, "You'll get warts." I said, "I've handled them, and I don't have warts." "You'll get them," she assured me.

For the first few days, a school teacher who had not yet left (school for the Indian children was out already, early in May) occupied the next room. Every evening her young man came to see her. There would be long silences, followed by sounds coming through the partly opened transom of what was apparently flesh slapping on flesh. My mother was both titillated and scandalized by such goings-on.

We spent several days on the whole quite happily, Mother stood the climate better than anyone could have anticipated. Then the heat intensified. The baby fell ill of a kidney or bladder complaint. She could not urinate and became feverish. Dr. Anna Israel Nettle, the Agency doctor, attended her and the condition cleared up in not much more than twenty-four hours, but my mother felt they had had enough; especially since I could not spend much time with them. Once again I saw my family wave goodbye from the window of a railway car.

IX   The Glowing Forge

WHEN THE TRAIN carried my mother and children away from me in Bakersfield, Harrington had stood at my side, earnestly endeavoring with his synthetic smile to make all things right. That had been a desolating moment. Now, standing alone on the station platform in Parker, I did not feel nearly so bereft. The baby was no longer a tiny infant, tearing at the heart; all three were in reasonable health; I was older, accustomed to being on my own, accustomed to separation, and I considered myself hard and cynical. None of

135

this really had anything to do with my lack of grief. Something new, a warmth, an unfamiliar excitement was stirring within me like the first flutterings of a child in the womb. I was secretly glad to be left alone to come to terms with—or at least to contemplate in a sort of rapturous peace—this as yet undefined emotion just emerging into consciousness. A meeting had occurred which was the pivot on which my life turned, although as yet I felt no prescience of the changes that turning would bring about.

My first Chemehuevi informant was Ruby Eddy, a woman of approximately my own age. With the exception of the Isleta policeman, Louis Abeita, she was the first person I had worked with who spoke fluent English, and I was delighted. But no later than our second interview, I began to be less than delighted with the quality of instruction I was receiving. She seemed to be speaking a sort of transitional Chemehuevi. She would give two forms of a quite common word, such as the term for "moon," one apparently an abbreviation of the other. Asked which was correct, she would usually say "it makes no difference," but when pressed stated that the longer form was "the old way." The people who habitually spoke this "old way" were, she thought, too old or too prejudiced against white people or too unfamiliar with English (or Spanish) to be of any assistance to me. There was, however, "one old fellow" who spoke the pure old Chemehuevi way, and who could also speak English, Spanish, and Mohave. Yes, she said in response to my eager questions, he had all his teeth and got along well with white people. But he was a man who "worked all the time." She didn't think he would want to take time off to talk to me. His name was George Laird. He was the Agency blacksmith and also worked at other jobs and cultivated his ten acre allotment. I was determined to try to secure this man's services as an informant. Ruby or somebody finally said, "Well, you can ask him"; and shortly thereafter someone—a man I'm sure, but

I don't remember if he was white or Indian—volunteered to walk over with me and introduce me.

The blacksmith shop was a windowless shack, stifling in mid-morning heat. George stood behind the forge and I first saw his face glowing in coppery light. That was the way I was to see it and to remember it all through the years, in actuality, in daydreams and in night dreams, lit by the gleam of coals in forge or campfire, by the light of kerosene lantern or lamp, or by the brief flare of a match as he lit his cigarette out-of-doors on a windy night, cupping his hands to shield the fragile flame: always the same beautiful contours, the same deep lines cut by sun and laughter in his dark brown skin, the same inimitable expression of kindness, intelligence, strength—and laughter lurking just below the surface.

Long, long afterward I asked him, "What did you think of me when you saw me there in the doorway?" He answered fervently, "I thought you were the prettiest woman I ever saw in my whole life." That, of course, was an inadequate attempt to express what he felt, not what he saw. I must have been anything but pretty standing there silhouetted against the blazing sunlight. I wore (I remember with great distinctness) a checked lavender and white gingham dress. I must have been pale from the heat. My hair was in a nondescript knot from which loose strands straggled damply down across my face. When he, in turn, asked, "What did you think of me?" I also answered inadequately: "I think I was afraid." Fear was certainly a component of emotions too complex to describe. There were also attraction and excitement, and a flash of what I can only describe as recognition.

The person who had brought me gave some sort of explanation of my presence. I put out my hand. George showed me apologetically that his was too dirty to shake. He laid aside his piece of hot iron and came outside the shack. He was, as he liked to describe himself, "built like the buffalo," with enor-

mous shoulders (now somewhat hunched from a lifetime of labor), the deep chest of a long distance
runner, slender hips and comparatively short, wiry
legs. I looked up at him, impressed by his massive
build. We spoke briefly. He would, he said, be glad
to tell me anything I wanted to know, but right now
he had a job of work to finish. If I wanted to get right
at it, his wife, Annie, spoke good Chemehuevi. He
would take me over where they lived and introduce
me. She wouldn't, he warned, have much to say in
English, but she would understand everything I
asked her. She was too bashful to talk much to
strangers. I was feeling bashful myself. I could not
believe that this man had agreed so readily to work
with me; and I wondered if the ironic gleam in his
eyes meant that he was secretly amused by my person
and my request.

George said he lived upstairs in a nearby building,
and we walked over to it, a few steps or a few
yards. I have no idea who or what occupied the ground
floor. He opened the door for me, and motioned me
to precede him up a flight of steps. He trod so silently behind me that I might have wondered if he was
following had I been less acutely aware of his gaze
fixed on my back. The thrust of the eyes can be as
potent as the thrust of the phallus.

We came out into a rather large, sparsely furnished room. There was a double bed covered by a
patchwork quilt, a chair or two, and I think a cookstove and table against the further wall. The woman
who occupied it seemed (to my eyes) much older
than the ageless man who said he was her husband.
She had a pleasant, intelligent face, and the thickened
torso and pendulous abdomen which often character-
ize Indian women in middle age, whether or not
they have borne children. George spoke to her quietly in Chemehuevi, explaining what I wanted and then
apparently overruling her objections. He again assured
me that she would understand every word I said,
then turned and went down the stairs. Annie nodded

her head at me and giggled like a very shy woman in an embarrassing situation.

I proceeded to make matters worse by the nature of my questions. Already with Ruby Eddy I had covered the basic questionnaire, the words for earth, wood, water, man, woman, sun, moon, etc. I wanted to re-hear these words from my promising new informant, but saw no point in having this woman repeat them. Having come armed with an elaborate questionnaire on relationship terms (based on a book or paper by Edward W. Gifford), I started in on it immediately; and received reluctant answers accompanied al-ways by that high, self-conscious giggle. (Once when George and I were rehearsing, as we loved to do, all the details of our first encounter, I asked, "What did Annie say about me?" George admitted she had not had a good impresssion of me. She had told him that I was trying to get her to say obscene words— that is, to say aloud the words she had once applied to persons now dead. "Was that all she had to say?" "To me. But she told some other people the white woman had come to take away her husband.")

I am not sure whether I was then living in the same house where I had stayed with my mother and the children or a different one. Probably it was the same, but somehow when I was with them I was oriented towards the cultivated fields, and after I be-gan to work with George I seem to have looked out only upon the vast, wild and aromatic desert. My quarters consisted of a room with adjoining screened-in sleeping porch. I believe it was in a building classi-fied as the Reservation Hospital, although it contained none of the equipment one associates with a hospital. Or part of it might have been used as a school for Indian children, though I do not remember any desks. It was a wooden structure with many empty rooms and bare floors on which one's footsteps echoed. At the far end of the hall was an apartment where Dr. Nettle lived with her husband, the Colonel, and a great slug of a neutered cat, the only cat I ever met in all my life with whom I positively felt no empathy. Dr. Nettle trapped mice for this beast and spent hours trying to induce it to exercise itself by playing with them, but the cat regarded her blandishments with complete disinterest.

Colonel Nettle was as off-beat for a man as Buster (I believe that was its name) was for a cat. He claimed to have held the rank of Colonel in the British army, serving in India and elsewhere, and in substantiation of this claim always wore immaculate whites and a sun helmet. He was a little old bantam rooster of a man, with red face and a fringe of white hair, and (at least in his imagination) he had been everywhere and seen everything. He could discourse on the appearance of a newborn African infant and on Hindu eroticism, as well as on any other subject that might be brought up or suggested. Certain townspeople in Parker had quite unkindly kept a record of how long he said he had remained in each place which he asserted he had visited. It figured up to at least one hundred and fifty years of adult life.

Dr. Anna Israel Nettle was considerably younger than her husband. She was also, I am positive, the homeliest woman I ever saw. All her life, she said, she had been possessed of an ardent curiosity about people, especially about the stranger and more off-color aspects of human existence. By her own account she had, by the time she was seventeen, wandered the corridors and peeped into the bedrooms of every brothel in her native eastern city (I do not recall what it was), obsessed by a morbid desire to know all that was to be known about a profession for which she lacked the physical qualifications. After she obtained her license to practice medicine, she had for a time been resident physician in a Florence Crittenden Home for Wayward Girls. According to Dr. Nettle, the girls received good care and the most advanced medical treatment—with the single exception that none of them was ever, under any circumstances, permitted to receive an anesthetic. It was the righteous belief of those in authority that illegitimate pleasure must be shown to bring inevitable pain. Some of the girls, Dr. Nettle commented with ghoulish relish, went raving mad while undergoing necessary operations.

Dr. Nettle was adept at palmistry and horoscopes. She cast my horoscope, utilizing all the data I could give her about the exact time and place of my birth. Then she examined my hands front and back, scrutinized both palms, and informed me that I was indolent by nature (which I already knew), that a break in my lifeline indicated an abrupt and radical change of course (which was already beginning to take place), and that I would die of a respiratory disease (which still remains to be seen). By this time, George and I were working together daily. I was so full that I had to spill over, and I spoke about him frequently to Dr. Nettle, commenting upon his phenomenal knowledge and abilities. She said he must have an unusually good horoscope "for an Indian." I neglected to ask her if Indians invariably chose to be born when the signs were inauspicious. When she went on to say that it would be impossible to cast it because "those people" seldom knew the date of their birth, I took a certain malicious pleasure in informing her that he had been born on March 3, 1871, and that he knew the date because it had been entered in the family bible of his father, Thompson Porter Laird. But she said the date wouldn't be of much use without the exact hour, and by this time she was looking at me a little too shrewdly, so I let the subject drop.

Dr. Nettle had a coterie of friends (whom I never met) with whom she liked to hold seances, during which the spirits manifested themselves by table-tipping and similar ghostly activities. On one occasion, she said, they had just succeeded in elevating the table several inches from the floor when someone looked out the window and saw the priest of the local Catholic church, known to be a deadly opponent of all such exercises, approaching to pay a call. The spirits proved obdurate, and it was harder to bring the table down than it had been to raise it. This story is possibly quite as factual as her account of medical practices in the Florence Crittenden Home—to say nothing of the Colonel's manifold adventures.

Although she considered herself a connoisseur of the occult, Dr. Nettle was totally insensitive to the immemorial powers, myths, and magics that whispered all around her. (In this she was not alone. I addressed the Parker Women's Club on the subject of "Wolf and Coyote Myths," and bored the good ladies into somnolence.) Nothing could ever spark Dr. Nettle's interest in the Chemehuevi culture, even then surviving only in intriguing memories, or the Mohave, which was still viable. When I repeated to her something that George had taught me (just what I can't recall—I think it was years later that he and I really got into the matter of shamanism) she remarked, "I wonder if these people could receive help from the Elementals?" Dr. Nettle was a great believer in Elementals. She said they clustered thickly about old battlefields. I gathered they were very dark and low grade spiritual beings, suitable to consort with Indians. Her vaunted interest in the human condition was at best cold and detached, and I do not believe she considered her Indian patients entirely human. I once watched her treating a Mohave girl in her early teens, suffering with a badly infected foot. The child apparently understood no English; she was in pain and frightened to the point of hysteria. When Dr. Nettle probed the wound, she screamed and hopped across the room on her uninjured foot, trailing gauze packing as the owl in Isleta had trailed rabbit entrails. The doctor, who had been gentleness itself with my own child, was impatient, contemptuous, not making the slightest gesture of reassurance. Maybe it had been her own notion to operate on the girls at the Home without anesthesia; they were not of a "primitive" race but they were "immoral." I think she may have envied their sexual experiences.

The day after we met, George came to work with me. I was almost incredulous, scarcely able to believe that he had kept his promise and had required no persuasion. Thereafter, I spent the greater part of each day in my room working with him. He must have continued on in his job as Agency blacksmith, but somehow he managed to get through with this task and all his other chores in very little time. One morning, however, he kept me waiting quite a long time. I said, "I thought you weren't going to come." He explained that he had got behind with his work because very early in the morning, just about sunup, as he had driven along the river road he had come upon rabbits playing in front of him, darting back and forth across the road, dodging and colliding and sometimes leap-frogging over each other. Of course, he said, stating a fact which must be obvious to me, he had had to stop his wagon to watch. My heart leaped as if it were one of the rabbits. For an instant, I sat in the wagon beside him, in the shimmering light and surrounded by the cool scents of early morning. Although he had never yet touched me, I could feel myself leaning against his shoulder, I could feel the solidity and warmth of his body. Never in my life before had I met a person who felt about animals as I did. My mother had often reproached me for the love and affection I, as a lonely child, had lavished upon my cats, speaking to them and to them as if they were people, made in God's image, instead of soulless beasts. To Harrington animals were objects to be named. Now I sensed that to George animals were "another kind of people." I found myself thinking: "I could love this man!"

I quickly discovered that no previous informant had had anything like George Laird's grasp of the problems involved in our work—and of course no previous informant had been inspired by an undeclared love to reveal to me all that I wanted to know. From the moment of our meeting, there was a rapport between us which went much deeper than a shared interest in words and myth, though at first it could only be expressed in such sharing. I was, as a matter of fact, quite ignorant in the field in which I was trying to work. Nothing Harrington had taught me had prepared me for the phenomenon of voiceless vowels. George patiently made sure that I heard them correctly and showed me that the unvoiced terminal sound was an integral part of each word. Also, when I asked my perennial question about "Coyote stories," he unhesitatingly began to tell me every myth he could remember, although the season was approaching high summer and the snakes were out in force. Years elapsed before he let me know that by this telling he had broken a strong taboo.

The room where we were beginning to partake of a deep spiritual and emotional experience opened only upon its sleeping porch and the hall. If there was an outside window, it remained tightly shuttered. Sheltered from direct sunlight, it was at all times dim and quiet. More and more it became for me a sanctuary, sharply demarcated from the rest of the house. When I ate dinner with the Nettles, their dining room seemed too bright for my eyes. The tablecloth was white, the Colonel's ducks were well bleached, the room was illumined by merciless sunlight or the stark brightness of electricity. Dr. Anna probably wore a white office coat, but I was too obsessed with her fascinatingly ugly face to notice or remember how she covered her thin body, lumpy in all the wrong places. Even our food was colorless. The abominable, grayish white cat did not care for mice or any form of red meat, but it had a passion for cream-style canned corn and minced clams. Dr. Anna bought these items by the case, and what was good enough for Buster was good enough for husband and guest. The conversation at Dr. Nettle's table was, one would have thought, somewhat darkly colored, but to me it seemed without substance. We had the Colonel's weird reminiscences.

His wife would draw him out, questioning him about various parts of the world, showing a deference she may or may not have felt. The doctor herself spoke of seances, Elementals, the moral lapses of young Indians (they had, she admitted, irresistible physical drives, "but I haven't been ordered to issue rations of saltpeter"), and the use of logarithms in working out horoscopes. In my abysmal ignorance of mathematics, I didn't know a logarithm from a hole in the head. Everything that was said struck me as pointless, shallow, and faintly offensive. My focus of reality had shifted.

Each evening I would find myself eager to get back to my own room, back to my vague dreaming in which George was always the central figure. Not that all my thoughts of him gave me pleasure. I did not like to imagine his going back to Annie, eating with her, perhaps laughing with her over things the white woman had said, then sharing the conjugal bed. What manner of sommersaults would my heart have done if I had known what his own dreams were at this period? In the late afternoon it was his practice to irrigate his corn patch, the minute parcel of land which constituted his sole real property—and even so was not entirely his, for it could not be disposed of without government sanction. He had recently installed head-gates at a cost of $300, and this was a matter for intense pride. Up until the time of our meeting, he had derived his deepest satisfaction from this field and its care. Now all was different. The land mattered not at all except as a site for an imagined drama. Leaning upon his hoe, he would see a child playing in the irrigation ditch, a child who might never be born, a little boy with light brown skin, his child and mine. This child was so real to him that he spoke to it, instructing it and comforting it—while I sat behind a closed door tormenting myself with the thought that he might be ridiculing me to another woman.

Eventually I would shake myself out of the daydream, look over my notes and write voluminously to

Harrington. I had to express my preoccupation with George in some way, and although I mentioned him far too frequently to Dr. Nettle, a certain discretion still prevailed in that quarter. In telling Harrington precisely what he wanted to know, I could recount much of what my informant had told me and thus in a way recapture our time together. I know that I received letters in return. They probably commended my efforts and certainly expressed pleasure at the quality of information I was securing. They must also have contained useful suggestions, practical advice on how to carry out my task, perhaps certain fossilized expressions of affection such as I may still have included in my epistles. The only sentence that I recall verbatim from any letter ever written by Harrington is "I dreamt that I was close to you last night and millions of germs were slaughtered." This gauche reference to an intimate relationship surely belongs to an earlier period, but in Parker it echoed distastefully in memory. In fact, everything personal about Harrington was becoming increasingly distasteful to me. I no longer idolized him nor feared him. He was still definitely a part of my existence but no longer central to it.

A sad but all too common occurrence broke the monotony of our days. A Mohave girl, aged about sixteen I think, the daughter of a man named Yellowfish, died of tuberculosis in the Indian Hospital at Phoenix and her body was shipped home to be cremated after the immemorial custom of her people. George invited me to attend the ceremony with him. "I'll come for you after dark," he promised, and his voice promised more than his words. I waited in my room with my heart beating very hard. I waited a long time. I became impatient, angry, then desolate and resigned. At last I turned off the light and lay down on my bed in the sleeping porch.

White moonlight flooded the desert and poured across my bed. I could hear the Mohaves singing their wild, yelping Coyote Song. The singing got louder and louder, never letting up for an instant. I think it was about midnight that the smell of burning flesh began to taint the air, blotting out the sharp, clean scents of the desert. The bright moonlight, the monotonous, alien yelping and the stench of human flesh consuming in the fire battered my senses relentlessly. Toward morning I dozed.

At sunrise I was awakened by a scratching on the screen. George's face was close to mine. He said in that slow, dark-timbered voice, "I didn't come for you because they opened the coffin right away when the train got in at three o'clock. The body got pretty ripe. I didn't think you could stand the smell." He never told me the real reason why he had not come. In all likelihood, the mourners had told him a white woman's presence would not be welcome. But why hadn't he simply come by and told me? I think that both he and I were afraid to let that powerful thing which lay between us develop too quickly.

Lying there in bed as George turned and walked away with his easy, rhythmic stride that seemed so deliberate and covered the ground so swiftly, I was suddenly overwhelmed by his *differentness*. I felt frightened when I remembered allowing myself to think, "I could love this man." His age (when one is almost twenty-four, forty-eight seems definitely over the hill), his unfamiliar, archaic background, his Indian wife, his dark voice and dark skin made the attraction seem bizarre and impossible. Yet hadn't I always, in spite of my mother's indoctrination, been attracted by darkness? When I was no more than thirteen I saw a young Indian walking in the streets of a Mexican town. He was, like all his fellows, dressed in ill-fitting white cotton garments which he had probably rented on the outskirts of the city, since it was forbidden to come into it *"sin calzones"*—without trousers. The grace of his body, the sculptured beauty of his face, had stayed in my mind for days and I had woven amorous fantasies about him and wondered what it would be like to follow him out into the hills.

Late one afternoon, when it was time and past time

for George to leave, he asked me if I would care to walk with him to see his stand of bees. I said "yes," and we left the building together. When we came to a barbed wire fence, he held the strands apart for me. Then we walked on very slowly. I looked back and saw that tall brush now screened us off from the Agency buildings. We came to a small shed that housed a stationary engine and pump. George asked me to wait while he oiled it and disappeared inside the shed. I waited. The sun had set. Overhead the sky was a pale inverted bowl, with not yet a single star. Suddenly I couldn't bear to wait any longer—it hadn't been more than three or four minutes, if that long, but it seemed an eternity. I had an awful picture of a man standing inside the shed watching, laughing at the white woman he had left alone on the desert. I turned and ran, rolled under the fence, and never stopped till I was back in my room.

Next morning he asked reproachfully, "Where did you go? I waited for you a long time."

Afterward, when we stood in a different relationship to each other, I explained that I had (oh, so wrongfully!) suspected him of laughing at me. "I would never have done that," he said, "I loved you too much." That quenchless gleam of humor in his eyes was, in part, a racial characteristic, since most Chemehuevis tend to find the world an amusing place. George, even more than others of his people, laughed inwardly at himself, at the world, and at the oddities of life in general. This was his armor against insult and perpetual disappointment, the bolster of his unfaltering sanity.

In the face of emotional turmoil, information kept piling up. I must have made a strong case in my letters to Harrington for the desirability of continuing this work. I do not think he read between the lines to discern my growing personal attachment to the informant. If he had, would it really have mattered? I doubt it in view of his attitude during the following months. Here is an aspect of Harrington's character which I cannot even pretend to understand. At any rate, I know that what I wrote from Parker whetted his appetite. He wanted to meet the man who was furnishing such copious information, to hear Chemehuevi for himself, and to check my work. Since he was now established in Santa Fé, he decreed that I should join him there and try my best to bring George Laird with me. This was my reprieve from what threatened to be an inevitable and unbearable separation. I felt I would die if George refused to go. This anxiety was needless. He agreed to make the trip as simply and quickly as he had consented to work with me.

Still no word of love had passed between us. The nearest thing to a caress was that one day George tapped my arm lightly with a flyswatter, pretending he had mistaken a mole for a fly.

George Laird
—Chemehuevi

X   Santa Fe: Summer And September

TO PREPARE FOR the journey George Laird bought a few new shirts and a wide-brimmed Stetson with a large, round crown. He packed his shirts, new and old, together with an old but seldom worn suit and several neckties, into his battered suitcase. He also packed his fieldglasses in their leather case. They were very good, originally quite expensive. He had bought them when as a much younger man he had worked rounding up cattle, so that he could spy out animals hidden by or entangled in heavy brush. He took

150

along his old-fashioned straight razor, which folded back into a mother-of-pearl handle, and his razor strap, shaving mug, and brush. Not to be left behind was his most treasured possession, his Colt's revolver, with its gunbelt and leather holster, already cracking with age. This weapon had been patented in 1871, the year of his birth, which seemed to him peculiarly significant. Its original handle had been broken and replaced, and even the new handle bore two notches. Later when we inspected it together, George told me that the notches had been carved by the gun's previous owner, a gunfighter of some renown. He himself, he admitted, had never shot anything nearer human than a maraudng coyote. (I must have been a bloodthirsty young monster, because at the time this was a source of some disappointment to me.) From some secure hiding place, he took a slender roll of bills and tucked it among his clothes. This was all that remained from money earned working in a manganese mine, a job that had terminated shortly before we met. It had been hard, dirty, lonely work, but the pay had been good. Part of it had gone to install the headgates, much of what was left over to relatives and friends— I have talked to an elderly man who remembers that when he was fifteen George Laird gave him a silver dollar. Then he gave away his stand of bees to a man who would take care of them, and possibly told someone else he could harvest the corn.

Having thus taken care of his worldly possessions, he announced to me, "I'm ready as brother." This was the expression by which he indicated readiness to embark on a trip or an adventure. I doubt if he said any formal good-byes, for the Chemehuevi language contains no words of greeting or farewell. Simply and without regret he walked away from his lifelong associates and from all that had previously constituted his world.

We boarded the train together early on a June morning. Conditioned perhaps by the segregated coaches to the presence of which I had been accustomed all my life, or influenced by I do not know what inward confusion, I asked the conductor as we stepped on board, "Do they allow Indians on this car?" His curt nod told me I had asked a foolish question and I felt shamed. George did not hold it against me. Only a brightened twinkle in his eye showed that he had overheard. Entirely without resentment, he began at once to show himself the perfect traveling companion.

Scores of jackrabbits watched the rain or leaped from cover at its approach. George said each one had its own hollow under a specific bush. There was a word in Chemehuevi which designated this "rabbit sitting place," equivalent to one's own vine and figtree in the realm of humans.

Soon we were laboring up the long grades from Wickenburg to Prescott. When he was much younger, George had hauled freight over the wagon roads that climbed these mountains. I don't know if he drove a "twenty mule train," but he had certainly managed a goodly number of mules. There was no vanity, no boastfulness in the man. Years later, from others not from him, I learned that he had also managed the whole operation and had been an employer of others. Now on the train he told me of a little old lady in a sunbonnet who lived in a house at the top of a long, steep gradient. Daily she leaned on her picket fence and watched the teamsters and their mules. One day she beckoned him over to her. "Young man," she wanted to know, "how come you git them mules to pull without cussin' at 'em?" She said that she had observed how he alone among the drivers did not curse and swear constantly. He explained—no doubt with grave courtesy and twinkling eyes—that mules pulled just as well without being cussed at. In fact, in all our years together I seldom or never heard George use profanity. I have the impression his father had taught him that "it warn't necessary." Thompson Porter Laird, Scotch with a dash of Cherokee, had run away from his home in Tennessee at the age of twelve to

join a westward-bound wagon train. Along with the
Bible in which, some thirty years later, he entered his
children's names, he brought other traces of gentility
which he passed on to his son.

That night we sat side by side in the chaircar, and
my head may have slipped against George's shoulder.
If so, he made no reciprocal gesture. The nearer we
came to Santa Fé, the more silent he became. He confessed that he was nervous at the prospect of meeting
Harrington, an apprehension due, as I clearly understood, to the fact that he was my husband. I attempted
to reassure him—but how could I explain to anyone
what Harrington was like? Especially since I didn't
know myself. George would learn from experience
more or less what to expect from him; but neither he
nor I ever really went beneath the surface of that repressed, masked and distorted personality.

Harrington had rented a small adobe house in Santa
Fé (or was it part of a larger house?—I dimly recall
a landlady). We had a livingroom, bedroom (one
only I think, since George slept on the livingroom
couch) and the luxury of a bathroom. I'm sure there
was a kitchen or kitchenette but I don't remember
doing much if any cooking in it, nor do I remember
that Harrington cooked his everlasting pots of mush.
He may have done so, but already his activities were
becoming dim and unimportant. It is my impression
that we took most of our meals out, usually in a restaurant with a Chinese proprietor, which we inevitably referred to as "The Chinaman's," though it was
considerably superior to the hole in a wall we had
called by that name in Los Angeles. The Taos informant, Manuel, came to that house in Santa Fé, but
I believe that Harrington interviewed him in the bedroom, leaving the livingroom to George and me. Since
the typewriter had been left in California, I had no
dictation to take, no copying or filing, and was supposed to devote my full time to working with the
Chemehuevi informant.

Now, at last, things were different between Harrington and me. From the time George and I joined him, I do not recall a single tirade, a single verbal attack. When we had last been in Santa Fé, an innocent statement that I would like to have a lawn for my children to play on had provoked a storm. Now I did not guard my speech at all, and my actions less and less; yet Harrington's reaction was limited to an occasional piercing or reproachful glance. And his self-control was not due solely to the presence of a valued informant, because even when we were alone in our room at night he did not take the opportunity to rebuke me. He respected the work I was doing on the Chemehuevi language and mythology, and felt that I was able to "get more out of the informant" than he could, but then I had done good independent work in Isleta without softening his attitude toward my frequent lapses from his ideal of wife and collaborator. Perhaps it was that at last I simply did not care anymore, and therefore was no longer vulnerable, or perhaps my greater independence intimidated him. In the days when we used to talk about such things, Harrington had always insisted that he had had a very happy, normal childhood, but in view of his adult character, I can only think that it must have been a time shadowed by fear and cruel repression.

For the first few days, George was watchful and puzzled. He had no clue to what Harrington was thinking or feeling and could not figure out the nature of our relationship. Then came the moment of truth. We were all in the livingroom. I was feeling under the weather with a cold or pain in my side or some other minor ailment. Manuel was absent, and Harrington was questioning George, rehearing some of my material. I wasn't so ill but what I had gone out to lunch, and on the way back I had violated all the standards set for me by buying a fiction magazine (*Cosomopolitan* or *Redbook,* or something of that ilk). Now I was lying on the couch reading it as openly and unashamedly as if I had been back in my parents' home. Harrington kept sliding glances at me but did not fly into a rage. However, the moment came when he could endure my idleness no longer. "If you're going to read," he said with rare restraint, "read something worthwhile." From the table beside him he picked up Sweet's *Primer of Phonetics* (a small volume bound in green cloth whose contents bored me excruciatingly) and tossed it to me. Now Harrington was not an accurate tosser, and I was never coordinated enough to catch anything. One corner of the book struck me solidly on the side of the abdomen. Both men leaped to their feet. Both exclaimed with a single voice.

George said, "Did it hurt you?"

— Harrington said, "Did it hurt the book?"

In the years after George and I had a family of our own, "Did it hurt the book?" became a family joke. Now George merely looked at the other man and shook his head unbelievingly. The incident had answered all his questions, not fully but sufficiently. From that time on he wooed me openly and I responded. He said at first that he asked nothing except to be my "loving friend"; but the words and caresses we exchanged when we were alone together, the glances that passed between us whether or not we were alone, were those of avowed lovers.

Summer passed in a dreamy, golden haze. It must have been near its end that we three went out for a social evening. I have no idea why Harrington consented to take the time away from his work, nor, for that matter, why any of us were invited. Perhaps a member of the Bureau of American Ethnology was a minor lion, perhaps it was *chic* in certain circles to have an Indian guest, perhaps Harrington and I were invited and I flatly refused to go without George. Anyway, there we were, quite excited and somewhat ill at ease in an unfamilar situation. There were other guests, whom I do not remember at all. Even our hostess' face is merely a pleasant blur. But it soon developed that she could see people's auras, and this made the occasion memorable.

Mine, she said, was rose and green. I don't recall which color appeared next to the body and which outside, but, however they were arranged, a lovely shade of rose blended into a lovely shade of green. Ever since I could remember, those had been my favorite colors, and I was childishly pleased to be (invisibly) enveloped by them.

The lady with the strange talent inquired about my religious belief. My head swam with myths which had become as real to me as the everyday world. I was fully persuaded that the beautiful aura was indeed visible to one who had eyes to see, and for months now I had felt myself borne along on currents of destiny, floating, as it were, between this world and some other. Yet I did not intentionally lie when, mostly from force of habit, I answered brashly, "Oh, I'm a complete materialist, I believe only in what can be scientifically proven."

Our hostess looked at me curiously. "That's odd," she said mildly, "I would have said you are perhaps the most spiritual person I have ever met."

I asked her, "Does Mr. Laird have an aura?" She focused her inward eye on him and saw it at once, very deep, very gorgeous: royal blue and gold. Whatever the order of the colors, they blended with mine—either the gold with the green or the blue with the rose. I gained the impression that one's congeniality with others depended upon the harmony of the auras.

Nothing was volunteered about Harrington. But when I pressed her, the seeress hesitated, then said "Gray." "What's the other color?" I asked, wickedly hoping for muddy brown. She shook her head. "Some people only have one color. His is gray. Sort of a steely gray."

There was no moon. We walked home under a vast darkness pricked with stars. Harrington was on my right, not touching me; George on my left, holding my arm. The unseen glory of our mingled auras arched around and above us. We laughed at everything. Like a child rejected by his peers, Harrington laughed when we did and tried to make witty remarks. But the things we laughed at were not witticisms. We crossed a small wooden bridge and I stepped in a hole. George caught me to him to steady me and we felt the beating of each other's hearts. Drunk without wine, I exclaimed, "I put my hole in a foot." We laughed immoderately, and that too became a family joke. (During that period we were accumulating jokes and sayings that would be remembered for a lifetime. Sad to say, many of them were at Harrington's expense.)

That summer and fall I alternated between a state of extreme vigor and well-being and a more or less pretended hypochondria. I think this was because I had never before been the object of a man's solicitous care and I wanted to exploit it to the full. Once I had a severe pain in my chest and insisted on seeing a doctor. Harrington, in his new docility, consented to call one. Since I had no decent nightgown, George was dispatched to select a proper garment. He came back, I remember, with something very pretty in blue. I put it on and he came in to see me. I indulged the unworthy thought that it would make him jealous to see me lying in Harrington's bed. But his manner was so kind, so genuinely concerned, that I was properly shamed. The doctor said my lungs were sound, the pain was probably due to a strained muscle and would go away in a few days. And that was that.

In September, the loveliest month of the year, George and I took the afternoon off. This was nothing new, for he refused to spend all his time cooped up and I often went with him on his rambles. This time the pretext was that I must learn to shoot his revolver. All afternoon he patiently directed my aim toward a certain spot on a large granite boulder; which, of course, I never hit. Overhead the sky was the clear pale blue of September in the high country. The floor of the desert was grayish white, grown over with gray-green, yellow-flowered rabbit bush. Our target boulder stood on the other side of a dry wash. The sun went down, its afterglow faded from the sky. When the twilight "crack between the worlds" opened briefly, we lay down together on the soft sand in the bed of the wash. George's coat was folded under my head, as it would be so many times in years to come. All excitement, all urgency of desire was washed away in an immense flood of mutal compassion.

As the stars came out we began the walk back to town, silent, close together, knowing that, in some way as yet unforeseen, we would manage to spend the rest of our lives together.

In a dark, narrow street on the outskirts of Santa Fé we became aware of a group of boys following us. Attracted no doubt by the noise of the revolver shots, they had made their wary approach and spied upon us. Now, emboldened by darkness, they came closer and hooted derisively. George said not a word. He turned on them, slowly, menacingly. In the night, his body loomed like a great bear standing on its hind legs. The boys fled precipitously. I do not think we were ever followed again.

My mind swarms with memories of the next few weeks. Time was elastic. As in a dream, experiences and adventures crowded into what was actually a short period.

George cut a poem out of the local paper which we declared to each other had been written "just for us." I remember one truly lovely line: "And the goldenrod is beginning to feather"—very appropriate, for indeed goldenrod was feathering along the ditches on the outskirts of the old, old town of Santa Fé; and I also remember the poem's closing quatrain: "So what care we if the nights grow cold?/Under one cloak we'll brave the weather./We're two jolly vagabonds under a hedge/And we're taking the road together." That was the refrain—"we're taking the road together." George was to carry this scrap of newspaper in his wallet till the years reduced it to a grayish powder mixed with dust.

One memorable evening we stood in a plaza tightly packed with people watching a group of mariachi dancers. The plaza was not large, the small wooden stage was not far from any part of the audience. Yet the performers seemed remote in space and time. They were tiny folk in archaic costumes with the stiff, stylized movements of puppets, and the voices in which they sang their Spanish folksongs were thin and reedy. The closing number was *"La Cucaracha,"* which delighted everyone, including George, with its familiarity. He towered above the crowd, most of whom were no taller than I. We stood close together, my head reaching just to his armpit, his out-stretched arm protecting me from the crush. We spared not a thought for Harrington, going over his notes in the brightly lit and stuffy livingroom.

On another evening we walked, just the two of us, under a pale cold moon surrounded by an enormous lunar rainbow. That, George said, was called in Chemehuevi "Dance Ring." My skin prickled at the concept of those innumerable ice particles as celestial spirit-dancers. We were following an abandoned narrow-gauge railway track, all grown up with grass between the ties. George balanced himself unfaltering on a rail, placing one foot directly in front of the other while accommodating his stride to mine. He assured me it was easy "if you don't look down at your feet," but I knew better than to try. Abruptly he detoured into the meadow beside the railbed, gathered a bunch of fragile white flowers (which might have been made of moonlight or frost except for their faint fragrance), and returning, thrust them into my hands.

I also recall wandering for hours under a blazing sun. I was hopelessly lost, George, as always, perfectly oriented. We were a little thirsty, and this gave us the excuse for exploring every small ravine where growth gave promise of water. We found nothing to drink, but we did come across an enormous horned toad, the grandfather of his kind. I had loved to play with "horny frogs" since childhood, but this one I looked at with new respect, for now I understood that he was a modern incarnation of his mythic ancestor and that back in "the time when the animals were people" his horny adornment had been a wreath of arrow flints tied around his head to prevent his being swallowed by Giants. As I held him, all puffed defensively, in my palm, he squirted a thin stream of blood from a suddenly reddened eye across my hand. Both George and I had heard all our lives that these creatures ould "shoot blood out of their eyes," but never having observed the phenomenon he had not believed in it, and I had been far too sophisticated (and ignorant) to give credence to such nonsense. Now we both stood corrected. As George wiped the small stain from my fingers with his handkerchief, he advised seriously, "You ought to wash your hands right away." Then he burst out laughing. "Now why did I say that when we've been hunting water a couple of hours?" This was one of our enduring jests of which Harrington was not the butt. George was always readier to laugh at himself than at anyone else. When he laughed at Harrington, it was without malice or meanness. Actually, he was more tolerant of the man than I was at that time.

George and I had another long day together when we went by train to attend a ceremonial dance at one of the Pueblos—which, I cannot remember. (Why do the names of Pueblos elude me? When we had been in New Mexico before, Harrington had taught me a phrase—in Taoseño, I think—which translated as "The meadowlarks are singing at . . ." At where? Again I forget the name in any language, also the phrase itself. I only remember that it had a lovely lilt, like the song of a meadowlark, and ended in "—te mirwe." Perhaps it was to this pueblo of the meadowlarks that my love and I went, but I can never be sure.) About midmorning I became carsick. I whispered to George that I was sick at my stomach and probably pregnant—which was foolish, for I could not possibly have been pregnant long enough to experience morning sickness. He whispered back that I was all right, I just felt sick because I had not smoked my usual cigarette after breakfast. We went out onto the rear platform and he rolled me a Bull Durham cigarette and lit it for me; and that, or the fresh air, cured my motion sickness. I attracted a few curious glances, bestowed partly because I was with George and partly because at that time it was still daring for a woman to smoke in public. (I did not particularly enjoy smoking, but had taken it up because it was pleasant and companionable to share a cigarette with George, because it made me feel closer to him and further from Harrington.)

The rest of the day is a confusion of color, rhythm, and blazing sun. I recall only dimly the plaza and the tiered adobe buildings that rose about it, the costumes and tireless movements of the dancers, the serious mass of Indian spectators in native dress and the wandering tourists. Back on the train after dark, exhausted by our day of sun and sight seeing, George and I both fell fast asleep and almost missed changing cars at Lamy. Later I wondered out loud what it would have been like if we had gone on east on that train and had simply dropped out of sight. George assured me we would have made out all right since he could earn a living anywhere; but neither then nor later did he put pressure upon me to make the break.

On one other occasion, we almost did not get back to the house where Harrington pursued his studies. That was the day we set out ambitiously to hike to the top of the mountain called (by Anglos, at any rate) Mount Baldy. All day we walked along a road that wound upward through wooded slopes. When we heard the clip-clop of hoofs or the chugging of an approaching Ford, we tumbled down into a brush-and vine-screened gully and hid like children—or Indians, not because we were particularly averse to being seen but just for fun. When the sun was low we reached the beginning of the real climb, the foot of the trail that led to the shelter hut on the mountain-top. A sign pointed two ways: 12½ miles back to Santa Fé and 12½ miles to the summit of Mt. Baldy. Illogically, I said I wanted to go on and spend the night on the mountain. George vetoed this, kindly but firmly: "No, hon. It ain't the time." I still can hear his voice, gentle, patient and a little sad. Then with that irrepressible spark of humor, he added, "You'd get cold without blankets."

Why wasn't it "the time" since we knew we were "taking the road together"? Why did George linger on in Harrington's employ, why did we still remain in a situation that was both awkward and humiliating? It was not George's fault, except that, sensing my unreadiness, he was willing to put up with anything to continue in my company. He said often enough that he could make a living anywhere we might be for me and for my children. The root of the whole delay was my deadly fear of my mother. Mother had a way of enduring my conduct just so far, then putting her foot down. I had been given to understand long ago that this putting down of the foot would involve getting complete custody of my children, and I believed she could and would do it if I went off to live in sin with a man I had picked up on an Indian reservation. While we were in Santa Fé I probably never spelled this out completely to George, but I didn't have to. He knew when I was ready to make a move and when I was not ready. (Ironically, all our delay, all my patience and planning would in effect come to nothing. The little girls would never live with me anyway, and I would pass my later years estranged from Awona, while enjoying a pleasant though not particularly close relationship with Elizabeth.)

On our way back we wasted no time and it was downgrade all the way. Just the same, it was past dark when we saw the lights of Santa Fé and possibly nine or nine-thirty when we staggered into town.

We had walked twenty-five miles that day without eating. The Chinaman's was still open. Euphoric with altitude, fatigue, and love, we went in boldly and ordered his most expensive meal.

Just as the big, tough, cow-country steaks sizzling on their hot platters were placed before us, George touched my foot with his. I looked up, and he gestured Indian-fashion, with lips and chin, towards a small table set against the wall. There sat Harrington, eating something out of a bowl while he scanned a newspaper propped up before him. The flavor went out of our day and out of the meal, which we finished in silence. When Harrington finished his soup or chile or whatever he was eating, he went directly to the cashier's desk and paid for it. It seemed that he studiously avoided looking in our direction, but we never really knew whether or not he had been aware of us.

Sometime in October, Harrington told me to ask George if he would accompany us to Washington. This time I was in no doubt as to what his answer would be.

XI   A Different Washington Winter

THE UPHOLSTERY IN the chaircars was (and for all I know, still is) red plush, that in the coaches, green. In the chaircars, the seats reclined, and had headrests and armrests, and there was a contrivance that could be extended for a footrest. In the coaches one had to sit bolt upright. But coach seats could be turned to face each other if people wanted to converse; and if one was lucky enough to get a whole seat for himself, he could curl up on it.

In thinking back to our journey to Washington,

one scene stands out, actually a composite of many
scenes. We are in a railway coach, George and I
seated side by side with me next to the window.
Harrington has turned his seat to face us, so that he
rides with his back to the engine. Beside him lie ma-
nilla envelopes, folders tied with red tape, and various
other parcels. On his face is a cheerful smile as he
makes conversation with his informant, bringing his
bits of information and witticisms down to the supposed level of that individual's comprehension. His
whole endeavor is, as always, geared to keeping the
informant happy. He had lost Manuel in the snowy
waste of the San Bernardino Mountains and has no
intention of losing George somewhere in the midwest.

Incredible as it seems, I sometimes think he may
have remained unconscious of the highly charged
emotional currents flowing between George and me.
Even so, he need not have feared his informant would
become bored en route. Until their age-old aboriginal
habits were abruptly changed by the brutal impact
of an invading culture, the Chemehuevis had been
great travelers. They had journeyed wherever their
swift feet would take them, for any reason and for no
reason, coming with the same outward calm and inner
excitement into the camps of friends, strangers, or
known enemies. On this trip, George would much
have preferred watching the passing scenery and
becoming acquainted with his fellow passengers to
listening to Harrington, although his native courtesy
kept him apparently attentive. George Laird had an
innate kindness and consideration for others—years after his death a woman who had known him spoke of
him as "the best mannered man I ever knew." Yet he
was never able to understand Harrington as a man,
and sometimes felt for him something not far from
contempt. In the months that followed, Harrington
became to him—as to me—more and more of a
cardboard figure, a tiresome encumbrance, and on
occasion, alas, a figure of fun.

In Washington, we had our old apartment, or one

so like it that it seems the same, with the single addition of a cot in the kitchen-livingroom for George. There every night he slept alone, while I slept just a few feet away stiffly balanced on the extreme edge of the double bed, awakening in an instant if the relaxation of sleep brought me into contact with my bedmate's body. But the days were ours to share. Now I was glad to be in a place where none of the wives of Harrington's acquaintances would come to call. This shabby apartment no longer seemed squalid. With complete reverence, I sometimes thought of it as "the upper room." Here we did our work faithfully. Naturally, we also made love, but quietly and decorously. There was in George, as in most of his Chemehuevi contemporaries as well as in the generation following, a certain puritanical reserve, due more, I believe, to generalized cultural shock than to direct indoctrination from missionaries or government schools. For example, we had been married for a number of years before he told me that Mythic Coyote's alter ego was his penis and not his tail, as in the version given in Washington. Our lovemaking was a natural and necessary background to the beginnings of our life together, but by no means the whole of it. More importantly, we talked, we continued to explore each other's thought and feeling, we began to make tentative plans for the future.

One morning, after Harrington left for his office I drifted into a sound sleep, to be awakened by the sound of George's singing. I don't think I had ever heard him sing before. I hastily went out into "his" room, the room where all that was vital to us transpired. He stood at the open window, watching the first big, loose snowflakes drift down through gray air into an unkept backyard. He was singing a snatch of song acquired during his three months' stay in a Protestant mission school—I was to learn that he never remembered any songs, even his own generations-old hereditary songs, except in tags and snatches. Now he sang: "Oh, come angel band!/Come and around

me stand!/Oh, bear me away on your snowy wings/
To my immortal home." He prolonged the o in "immortal," giving the word a peculiarly eerie sound.
His face was wrapt, as in the act of love. I had
never seen him so blissful, so completey carried out of
himself with numinous joy.

Although I shared my mother's delight in food,
she had never taught me to cook. She said I lacked
patience to learn; I felt she lacked patience to teach.
Housework which she hated and cooking which she
loved were activities not to be encumbered by a
child who was all thumbs. Closely supervised by
Harrington, my culinary skill had increased a little
but not much. Now with a man of my own to cook
for, I taught myself. More than that, I began to perceive the sacramental nature of the preparation and
sharing of a meal. George was appreciative. He had a
Mohave saying which he quoted at the close of every
meal. It meant, "Oh, how good is the white man's
food!" This encouraged me enormously.

One evening I served a roast, baked sweet po-
tatoes, and creamed turnips. Harrington helped himself several times to the turnips. Very much on his
good behavior, he complimented me: "These po-
tatoes have a very delicate flavor." George shook his
head, tried to restrain himself, and burst into laughter.
I joined him. Harrington laughed too, never asking the
reason for our amusement. I always thought, through
the years that I was with him, that his mind was
simply too occupied with other matters to sort out sen-
sory impressions. Now I wonder if he did not suffer
from an impaired sense of smell. His tastebuds were
intact; he could distinguish between bitter, sweet,
sour, and salty. But perhaps his perception of odors
was deficient or partially lost. This might account
for his willingness to economize by eating spoiled
food. My own grandmother, losing her sense of smell
in her eighty-ninth year, was discovered by a horrified
granddaughter cooking an over-ripe chicken, than
which nothing is more odoriferous.

Because George was interested in everyone and made friends with everyone, the people around us began to assume a little more form and substance. Particularly the middle-aged Jewish couple who kept a neighborhood grocery store directly across the street. I shopped there occasionally, Harrington very seldom, but George was in and out almost daily chatting with the proprietors and playing with their cat. I worried a little about what they would think of us. George assured me it would be all right. He came in one afternoon grinning broadly. The couple had worked out their own completely satisfactory explanation of our *ménage à trois*. They had invited "Mr. Laird and his sister" over to taste the sacramental wine they had made. I put on my coat and we walked across the icy street. The Steins (or whatever their name was) locked their front door (although it was a little early to be closing!) and ushered us ceremoniously into their living quarters at the back. We stood around the dining table holding small glasses of a clear red liquid having the sweetness and consistency of pancake syrup and (to us) no perceptible alcoholic content. It was a lovely, a memorable moment. After we had praised their accomplishment, and chatted briefly about the terrible weather, and taken notice of the cat, we went home to stand before a mirror with our faces laid together. For the first time we noticed that there was between us what might have been called a "family resemblance." George was very dark, I very fair. But forehead, eyes and cheekbones—indeed all the contours of our faces except my prominent "Chaddock nose"—were markedly similar. We felt a new surge of love and kinship. George was and has remained my father, brother, lover, husband, and, above all, my friend.

On yet another wintry day George came back from visiting or shopping across the street. He was laughing, holding up a hand raked with claw marks and dripping blood. "Stein's cat got me good," he explained; then added, apologetically, "It looked so cute, lying there on its back!" Even while I was exclaiming, "You'd better put something on it right away!" and "I wish we had some iodine!" and George was rinsing his hand off under the faucet and declaring, "Stop worrying! It's all right," I found myself caught up in an emotional storm. Broken phrases from a forgotten hymnal streamed to the surface of my mind: "Precious blood," and "Whose blood was shed for me . . ." Why should I be so moved, so shaken by the sight of a very little blood? I wasn't one of those silly persons who faint at the sight of blood. And George wasn't the suffering Christ; he was just a man who hadn't been smart enough to avoid touching the belly of a mischievous cat, upturned in treacherous invitation. Yet somehow he *was* my savior, and I had seen for the first time his bright blood flowing. I can't at this moment remember seeing it again, though he must have sustained numberless cuts and scratches in the course of our life together. But the shedding of blood is symbolic; this man would uncomplainingly give his life to hard and frequently uncongenial toil for me and for our children.

No more than in Santa Fé did George consent to a completely sedentary existence. He fully intended to take advantage of this once-in-a-lifetime opportunity to explore the nation's capital. We went together to see the outer environs of the White House (it is my impression that sheep still grazed on the lawn). We rode streetcars interminably, and sometimes on Saturday nights we walked along Seventh Street, where a rising tide of blackness was prophetic of things to come. We visited the Library of Congress and, by great good fortune, were allowed to hold in reverential hands the slim, timeworn brown volume that contained a picture of George's ancestor, Black Turtle. This redoubtable lesser chief is depicted, together with two or three Chemehuevi women, boldly standing on the deck of a ship (a side-wheeler, if I remember correctly), which was exploring the navigability of the Colorado River.

George went alone one day to see the interior of the Capitol. I was in bed with a cold. During this whole winter I had not a one of the terrible boils that had plagued me during my previous stay in Washington, but I still came down with colds. Even George's robust health cracked a little under the strain of confinement and cold, dirty city air. Towards spring he suffered from infected eyelids and a doctor prescribed Fleischman's yeast—people were just becoming vitamin-conscious. Nothing fazed Harrington, not even the long exile from fieldwork. Now that George was with us, we had better food and consequently he suffered from fewer stomach aches; occasionally, he had the sniffles and looked pale for a few days, but nothing interfered with his work.

A favorite haunt of ours (George's and mine) was Rock Creek Park and its zoo. We sympathized with a bored and lonely chimpanzee. The keeper told us he had been trained to eat at a table, using knife and fork, and every day at a certain hour visitors had gathered around to watch and exclaim. The chimpanzee had enjoyed being the center of attraction. But during wartime he was forced to eat in private, because of public protest at the waste of food, and now in peacetime the practice had not been resumed. Kept indoors (because of the cold) in a too-small cage, the unfortunate beast had nothing to occupy his attention except the visitors who stared at him. However, he was not as far from the human condition as these people may have thought. Once we saw him make sudden amorous advances to a woman visitor—who promptly screamed and took refuge in her escort's arms. The zoo also held a cheetah. This great cat purred thunderously when a certain friendly and courageous visitor scratched its belly—unlike its small relative, it made no sudden movement of the claws.

But neither George nor I could stand for long the sight of animals in close confinement. We preferred the illusion of wildness outside in the almost deserted park: the rushing stream rimmed in ice and the gloomy, unkempt woods. There was a small summer-house, empty and forlorn. We must have visited it before the full onslaught of winter, for I remember that sodden brown and yellow leaves swirled around it in windows on the muddy ground. Standing there with George beside me, I began to weep with pre-monitory loneliness and grief, tasting the bitterness of a separation that would not occur for many years.

It was Miss Clark who had told us we must be sure to visit Rock Creek Park. I think she must have had pleasant girlhood memories of that rustic place. Miss Clark was the sole friend who welcomed me back to Washington. We were still frequently invited to the "little gatherings" at her home, and George was in-cluded in the invitations. Miss Clark was wiser, more perceptive and more tolerant than I then realized, and in retrospect I am sure that, from the moment she saw us together, she knew how things stood between George and me. She treated him always with exquisite consideration. I can still see her birdlike figure, head cocked to one side, bright black eyes glinting, as she looked up—far up—into George's face and asked Mr. Laird's opinion about this, that, or the other thing. He always responded gravely, deliberately, and thought-fully, giving his viewpoint or just as deliberately telling her he couldn't say because he didn't know; and al-ways his eyes held that secret gleam which implied the whole conversation was an amusing game, which would lose its point if not played out as if it were se-rious.

Usually included among our fellow guests were Harrington's rather dull Indian colleague (Huron, Iroquois, or whatever) and Miss Clark's next door neighbors, a brother and sister, both unmarried, both so bony, sparse, and taciturn that they were more like an artist's stereotype of New Englanders than flesh and blood people. No evening was complete without a ref-erence to this neighbor's wonderful success in growing roses and a hint about his secret horticultural method, which he would reveal to no one.

Both the cultivator of roses and the ethnologist were more than a little smitten with Miss Clark. They were even courting her in their respectively reserved and sluggish manners. This was fairly obvious, but she confirmed it to me in the moments we spent alone together in her kitchen. I didn't care much for the Indian as a man, but because of my own situation I would have been delighted if they had made a match of it. Miss Clark vetoed this firmly. "No, I wouldn't consider him. I don't want to spend the rest of my life nursing a hypochondriac." When this man took his leave, she made it a point to call after him sharply, usually just as the door was closing, "Don't forget your overshoes!" "If I don't remind him," she explained, "he'll leave them on my front porch. Then he'll get his feet wet and catch cold. Then he'll say it was my fault."

Apropos of this, George and I made up a saying between us: "There's nobody as soft as a soft Indian." Harrington thought this amusing and repeated it on occasion.

For a time, Miss Clark confessed to me, she had regarded the New Englander more favorably. Their backgrounds were similar; she liked his roses, got along well with his sister, and had been lonely since her mother died. But early one morning, happening to glance out a back window just after the milkman's wagon clattered by, she had seen her suitor on his knees with broom and dustpan, collecting the still steaming manure dropped by the milkman's horse. In these days of intense interest in ecology, recycling, and a return to nature, such an action would be wholly admirable—that is, assuming that milkmen still drove horses. To Miss Clark, it seemed rather a disgusting explanation of the vaunted "secret"—I think she had hoped for something esoteric—and revealed a streak of parsimony too strong even for her frugal nature. This account prompted me to suggest once more that at least some of Harrington's peculiarities might be due to his origins. Miss Clark disagreed. Yes—perhaps it is sheer coincidence—the only man I ever met whose eccentricities approximated Harrington's, a man met many years after Harrington and I had parted, was also descended from an old, respected, inbred New England family.

The winter solstice, the turn of the year, marked another turning point in my life or rather, the beginning of the final shaping of that turning which had begun when George's eyes met mine in the gloom of a blacksmith shop. It was about then that we began to put into words our still nebulous plans for marriage, for a permanent and settled life together. I was child enough to be excited by the approaching Christmas season. I do not know how George had celebrated previous Christmases, or if they had meant much to him one way or the other, but he caught my enthusiasm. This proved to be the warmest, happiest holiday time I had experienced since my marriage, as different as possible from the dreary visit to the ranch in the Simi Valley.

Curiously, it was also at this season that the old Harrington surfaced briefly, and, so far as my recollections go, for the last time. Since moving to California, my mother had substituted an orgy of holiday fruit buying for her previous orgy of cake baking—not that our home was ever without a homebaked cake, it was just that the ritual twelve were no longer baked for Christmas. Among the seasonal fruits, standing out as delicious and exotic, were Japanese persimmons. Mother piled them in a cutglass bowl and placed them on the sideboard to mellow in winter sunlight. Shopping for Christmas delicacies on a cold and cloudy late afternoon, I was delighted by the sight of a glowing heap of this fruit. Overcome by nostalgia, I bought some, perhaps half a dozen, on the spot. Harrington had tagged along on this expedition and saw the price I paid.

"My mother," he pontificated with justifiable out-

rage, "never bought fruit till it got down to two cents a pound."

"Your mother," I retorted, "never bought fruit in the winter in Washington, D.C."

This flippant answer seemed to bewilder Harrington, and he did not pursue the subject. In the old days, it would have been the start of a battle royal, terminating in tears on my part and a prolonged fit of sulking on his.

I bought velvet dresses for the little girls (out of my own money probably) and George helped me wrap and mail them. And for him, most definitely out of my own money, I bought a small camera with which we could take pictures of each other on our sight-seeing expeditions. I do not recall buying anything for Harrington, and am quite positive that Christmas morning came and went without my receiving a gift from him.

Almost two weeks before Christmas, George purchased a Swiss-made wristwatch for me, the first I had ever owned. Unable to wait, he gave it to me immediately. At first I kept it hidden from Harrington, wearing it only in his absence. One day, growing careless, I left the closed red velvet case containing my watch on the windowsill in the room George shared with the kitchen stove and the combination work and dining table. Later George said to me, "*He* saw it. I wonder what he thought? I wonder why he didn't ask what was in it?" Both of us wondered still more when the day came, as it inevitably did, on which I forgot to remove the watch before Harrington came home. I remember that he sat at the table writing, slewing his eyes over for frequent, furtive glances at my wrist, but never asking a question nor making a comment. What indeed did he think? Did he suspect that George had given it to me? Did he think that in a fit of extravagance I had bought it for myself? Was he afraid of what my answer would have been if he had questioned me? What would he have done if I had announced forthrightly, "George and I are in love and plan to spend the rest of our lives together. This watch is his gift to me, in lieu of an engagement ring?"

The rather sad mystery is how I could have been so long and so closely associated with this man without learning what he really thought about anything except the work which absorbed him and his fellow scientists, of whom he had a consistently poor opinion, or what his inmost feelings were, or even if he had such feelings. Once (this must have been weeks or even months after Christmas) I recklessly tried to prod him into some sort of angry reaction. It was in the evening after the table had been cleared. Harrington sat at it writing, George was lying on his cot. I rose from my chair, went over to George and said, "Move over. I'm tired, I want to lie down too." He did move over and I lay beside him for a few moments. I only succeeded in embarrassing him and myself; Harrington never missed a stroke of the pen.

All my early memories of Harrington are action memories. I see him striding along, too fast for me to keep up; bustling about, packing and unpacking voluminous notes and meager camp gear; asking persistent questions in Spanish of suspicious strangers as he endeavored to locate informants; sitting listening with cupped ear and strained smile; pacing the floor and literally tearing his hair as he dictated letters or conclusions, or merely excoriated all other ethnologists for their stupidity and venality, all bureaucracy for its unreasonable demands, or himself for the sin of procrastination. Then George comes into the picture, and him I remember in the greatest detail: his eyes, his expressions, the corners of his mouth, the way he moved and spoke; while Harrington has become all but invisible. I cannot recall his face at all during this time, except that occasionally it bore a sourly reproachful expression. All that I really remember of him is a vague picture of a man writing, writing, writing.

What did he write so incessantly? It is my impression that when not engaged in recording words directly from an informant, he mostly busied himself in what he called "slipping" the material. Actually he was card-indexing, but since he used his specially printed slips of ruled paper instead of cards, "slipping" was perhaps the more accurate term. Each sentence, specialized terms, phrase or statement was filed under its subject, after a separate slip had been made for every word or significant part of a compound word, also for all peculiarities of construction, etc. All these were necessary steps toward final analysis and the preparation of the material for publication. But Harrington tended to get stuck in the preliminary stages. He did not, as I have already said, wish to publish anything till it was complete, and deep in his unconscious there must have been the determination that it would never be complete and therefore never exposed to other eyes. Also, for a man who was so absorbed in words, their minute nuances of sound, their complex derivation, he was peculiarly insensitive to the cadences of English prose. His words moved as awkwardly as his body, and far more laboriously. Composition was a dreadful chore. Ignorant though I was, painfully uncertain of grammatical structure and often of spelling, I rather enjoyed writing, or trying to write, once I had broken out of a state of inertia. My lifelong love affair with the English language was already in progress. But Harrington, who loved *words* more than flesh and blood, could only find pleasure in stringing them together when he attempted to write poetry—and that was a luxury he seldom permitted himself. Therefore, he tended to engage in "busy work," satisfying his conscience while putting off the dread act of producing a manuscript.

Sorrowful and monotonous, the last weeks of January blended into February. There were gray skies above and dirty gray snow underfoot, alternately thawing into slush or freezing into icy ridges. On one of these dark mornings, Harrington having departed, I came out to find George lying on his cot, dressed but unshaven. He did not speak or move, or acknowledge my presence in any way, and merely made a slight negative motion of the head when I asked if he was sick. I knelt beside him, frightened, bewildered, almost heart-broken, because I thought I must have given offense. He did not respond to my touch. But when I began to cry, he said with great effort, his voice coming from some far off, dismal place, "I get this way sometimes." This way my first experience with one of his rare seizures of melancholy. These recurred at long intervals and with lessening force during the years of our life together, and ultimately, towards the end of that time, disappeared or became unnoticeable. At the time I lacked the empathy to perceive the roots of this sadness. I now believe that, like his ironic sense of humor, it was bound up both with racial heritage and personal history. He had lived from the time of his grandfather, Black Turtle, when the ways of the People were vivid in memory and sometimes still practiced, on through a time of forced acculturation. The slightly older companions of his adolescence had fought skirmishes with the Mohaves and had been familiar with ancient rites and skills. Now these young men were long since dead of imported diseases or of the malaise that accompanies loss of identity. He himself had never been allowed to use his considerable ability to fully compete in the white man's world, and had at last accepted settlement on a reservation which was dominated by the Mohaves. His white father had spoken to him of the world of desert rats and mountain men, but this world too had quickly vanished. His sisters had accommodated themselves to the ways of Mexican settlers, but even this alien culture would soon be dominated by the arrogant newcomers who called themselves Americans. What Ruby Eddy had told me of George was true: he spoke fluent Chemehuevi, Mohave, Spanish, and English. And it was also true that his life experience had bounced like a pingpong ball between these four diverse cultures and the equally diverse culture of the earliest pioneers.

In my self-centered youth, I did not understand the vicissitudes and pressures to which this man had been subjected. That day in Washington I only knew, when

he at last came back to me from his place of infinite
sorrow, that I could not bear to lose him and that I
would not feel safe till all our plans were spelled out
as definitely as possible.

With this in view, I said rather tentatively, "I'll have
to go back to California and stay till I get my divorce.
And I suppose you'll have to go to Parker to arrange
for yours."

"I don't need no divorce," George countered, "I
never been married." Then with all the familiar love
and laughter back in his eyes and voice, he added,
"I never wanted to marry any woman till I met you."

That simplified things, but only partially. I still had
to have my marriage dissolved, and, if I was to
keep my children, I needed my parents' shelter and
cooperation till this was accomplished. I would have
to return to their home and play it by ear from that
point. But how should we even go about making the
trip to California! I had virtually no money, George
very little. We agreed that from now on he would
save his meagre wages, and that we would try to
stick it out till Harrington was about ready to pull up
stakes in the spring.

XII   All Across America

THE VERNAL EQUINOX brought a touch of madness. George and I became obsessed with the plan of driving overland to California. It was a wild idea, a thoroughly impractical notion. Cross-country driving was still considered something of an exploit, not to be undertaken lightly. And, of course, we had no car. But gradually a daring project took shape in my mind. I was beginning to wonder if the work I had done for Harrington might not have been worth more than I had received for it. He had thoroughly impressed me

179

with the belief that all my exertions had been no more than simple wifely duty; and moreover my thoughts in regard to our entire relationship were now filled with guilt and confusion. Nonetheless, I wondered and went on wondering. A Chevrolet touring car was to be bought for three hundred dollars. George agreed with me that it might be fair to ask Harrington for that sum, and then no more forever. That was the way I put my proposition, bluntly and harshly, because inside I was so very fearful. We stood facing each other. I was trembling, but my voice was firm and high-pitched and icy. "George and I intend to drive back to California," I said. "I want you to give me three hundred dollars to buy a car. I won't ask you for any more money."

That old familiar scowl darkened Harrington's face. This was the last time I was to see it; in fact, I don't remember seeing him at all after that, though we continued living in the same close quarters for weeks. He looked sick and angry, but if he said anything at all, I don't recall it. He gave me the money—it is my impression that he had it on his person, but he may have handed it to me later.

Using my own money, I shopped for the journey. I bought a black skirt and two smocks, one rose, the other green. Miss Clark said, "Mrs. Harrington, you are a good shopper. You know how to get good value at a cheap store." (But the smocks were not color-fast. Under the western sun they soon faded to white across the shoulders.) Miss Clark volunteered to accompany me on a later shopping expedition. This time we went to a better store. I tried on hats and she prevailed upon me to buy one which "definitely did something" for me. It was a finely woven dark blue straw with a modest wreath of pink rosebuds and dark green foliage around the crown. It cost the outrageous sum of seventeen dollars—and was destined to be known to the Laird children as "mama's hat" and to gather dust for many years on a closet shelf in our little house in Poway.

One of the hardest things was to write my mother about the projected trip. She wrote back immediately, imploring me to reconsider. She said I would lay myself open to "charges of white slavery" and would surely be arrested "under the Mann Act." These rather incoherent admonitions were her way of serving notice that she suspected George and I were lovers. I wrote back coldly that her fears were nonsensical; that the Mann Act referred to the transportation of females; that the car belonged to me and I would be doing the transporting.

All this time I went about biting my lips and holding my breath, amazed at my own cruelty and ruthlessness, amazed that a woman who was so wicked could feel so pure and free.

What with one thing and another, when the day finally came, when I had taken delivery of the car and our belongings were packed, we got off to a late start. It was mid-afternoon. The sensible thing would have been to leave early the next morning. We did not want to be sensible. We could not endure another night's, another moment's delay. The month was May of 1920. It was almost precisely a year since I had gone to Parker.

I have no recollection at all of telling Harrington good-bye. I cannot say whether we parted courteously or on bad terms, or whether or not anything was said about writing. Somewhere in my memory a ghostly figure of a man stands looking after me, but that may be sheer imagination.

One reason for our delay in starting was that belatedly I discovered that the state of Maryland would not honor a District of Columbia driver's license, which I had obtained with only slightly more formality than that attendant upon securing my first California license. Strictly a self-taught driver, I was highly apprehensive of the Maryland test. Rather than try it, rather than risk frustration and further delay, we took a look at the map and decided to go around Maryland, dipping down through Virginia and West

Virginia. This lengthening of the journey coincided with our shared desire that it would last forever. Someone, perhaps the automobile salesman, warned against the roads in West Virginia. No matter. I had driven before on bad or virtually nonexistent mountain roads.

That first evening we only went a little way beyond Alexandria, Virginia. We had no desire to drive on into the night. Spring was odorous around us, the dogwood was in bloom, George and I were actually on our own together. There was no place private enough for camping, so we spent the night at an old-fashioned southern home converted into a wayside inn for the motorists who were coming that way in increasing numbers. Since the car was registered in my name, we had decided in advance that George would register us as "George Harrington and wife." If this disturbed him, he didn't show it. I think it tickled his sense of humor. Our room was large, with a big, comfortable four-poster bed and a commode with wash basin, pitcher, and chamberpot tucked away behind doors.

This night was memorable because it was our first together, the very first time that we could fall asleep in each other's arms and wake together in the morning. We were very decorous. I wore a long-sleeved nightgown and George slept in his long underwear.

A night or two afterward dusk found us thoroughly lost in the wooded hills of West Virginia. We had maps and elaborate printed travel directions, but they were the sort that read "right turn at large oak tree, then left at pigpen." We stopped the car and futilely tried to make out our way. An old woman was watching us from the porch of her shack. Although it was so nearly dark, she still wore a black sunbonnet. George said, "I'll ask her," and crossed the road to her armed with the names of two towns which couldn't be far away. He came back to tell me that she thought it was "'bout five mile" to one of these, but couldn't say how to get there, never having traveled to "furrin' parts." It was coming on to rain. We pulled the car off the muddy track, put up the storm curtains and spent the night under dripping trees. Sleeping together on the back seat, in pitch blackness with droplets of rain finding their way inside the ill-fitting curtains, we were like two unborn souls in the womb of the world. There was no feeling of being cramped, only of peace, isolation, and eternity. In the morning, I slid down a bank and washed my face and hands in a roiled stream. Then a veil drops, and I don't remember if George cooked something for breakfast or if we went on to eat in the illusive town. I think we bought our cooking utensils later on: an iron frying pan, a small pot for heating cans of beans or corn, and a coffee pot.

There must have been nights spent with Harrington in the Ford, but they are all blocked out. Although I do remember well enough certain awakenings to stiffness, grime and icy chill, to a cold breakfast of leftover mush or of something eaten out of the can. It was on one such morning, up on the Ridge Route, that I had made so bold as to throw away a damaged can of corn and call down vengeance on my head.

The trip George and I made together all the way across North America in the beautiful spring of 1920 was a joyous adventure, not without its rough spots, but even those shine in memory with an enchanted light.

Leaving West Virginia, we veered northward, back toward the route we had originally planned. So far as possible, we avoided cities. To our country hearts they seemed hazardous. I think it was in Grafton, Pennsylvania, that we experienced a particularly panicky moment. We were driving on a railway track that ran down the middle of a street. Suddenly a train approached headon. I thought I wasn't going to be able to pull the car free of the rails.

My next clear picture is of a group of people sitting around a stove. We are in a small hotel on the outskirts of Columbus, Ohio, discussing weather and road conditions, and the rain is pouring down. I remember that the men thought driving to California was a harebrained plan. One said positively, "You'll never make it. You'll run out of paved road about ten miles out of town and stop. Bogged down." We bogged down, all right, how many times I can't say. Sometimes we dug ourselves out, sometimes we had to hire a farmer to pull us out of a particularly deep mudhole. But for the most part we just kept going, the gallant, tinny little car chugging along with its running boards, dragging in the mud. Later, rattling along on high, dry ground, the results of this ordeal showed up in a general looseness of parts of the engine. George cut gaskets or washers or whatever out of tin cans with my manicure scissors and made his own repairs. He hadn't learned to drive yet, he'd never been much around automobiles, but he had a natural genius for machinery.

It was raining still in Des Moines. We took a room with bath in a cheap hotel and washed some of the mud off. I remember the tin bathtub and the low-powered electric light bulb. Every detail is clear, because this is the first time we completely undressed in each other's presence. I scrubbed George's back. His skin, unexposed to sun and wind, was no darker than my deeply sunburned forearms. This was reason for delight. At that time neither of us cared whether we were Indian or White; we just wanted to be alike.

In St. Joseph, Missouri, after all those days of rain and heavy mud, the sun shone. In the hotel we struck up an acquaintance with a couple traveling—actually tramping and hitch-hiking—west. We walked with them down to the river to see an old sidewheeler, and sat together at the family-style dinner table for our evening meal, and later spent hours talking in our room. They were older than I, much younger than George. George and I were fascinated by their adventures, and we formed a congenial foursome. Since their destination was the same as ours, the proposal was inevitably made that we join forces. They offered to pay for their own food and more than half the gas, in return for the ride. We said we would have to think it over.

Our friends withdrew and we consulted privately. It was a moment of consternation. We couldn't (or thought we couldn't, which came to the same thing) tell them that we were not married. We had the nightmarish vision of driving up in their company to my parents' home, with them still under the impression that we were man and wife and that George's name was Harrington. Also we did not want anyone intruding on the all-too-brief time we were sure of having together. George said, "I'll have to tell them 'No,' but I sure hate to." We told them. They argued, "Why? Why? We'll pay our share, we'll pay more than our share." In the morning, we got up very early, hoping not to see them again. But when we drove off in the gray dawn our would-be companions were standing forlornly on the sidewalk, packs on backs, hoping till the last moment that we would relent. George made a sheepish gesture of farewell. To leave them there went against his generous nature, against all his habits and traditions. He did it for my sake. Left to himself, he would have worked out a way to take them along.

We had sunlight all the rest of the way. I should have been glad because George loved it and it made the trip easier, but it saddened me, because the brightness reminded me that every day brought us nearer journey's end.

One night we stopped to eat in a country grocery store with two tables provided for diners. I said, "I think I'll just have a bowl of soup," and George said "Same for me." The proprietor answered somewhat reprovingly, "It's kinda late in the season for soup." Then reaching down a can of chile from a shelf, he conceded, "I reckon I could heat ya up some chile soup." And breakfasting in a similar place, my request for breakfast food was answered by, "We're all out of everything but apple." Thereafter, for the rest of our time together we referred to western Missouri and all of Kansas as "the pie for breakfast belt" or "the chili soup zone."

The farther west we drove, the more noteworthy our District of Columbia license plates became. This being an election year, men stood outside wayside general stores and filling stations, commented on where we came from, and called out after us, "Who's going to be the next President?" George always shouted back loyally, "Johnson of California." Together we were beginning to take an interest in politics.

At last we climbed back into the high country. George was happy, but I was a worrier. One afternoon we camped under juniper trees beside a deep ravine, probably somewhere in Arizona, for I remember that the map was providing inexorable evidence that we hadn't too much farther to go. There we were joined by a loner, a drifter traveling in a battered pick-up truck. This was the kind of masculine companionship George had been missing for many a month. The two men sat late by the campfire after I had gone to bed. Conscious that our journey was drawing to its inevitable end and our future uncertain, I writhed in jealousy because George spent time with this stranger which he might have been spending alone with me. He was always the calm one, taking each moment as it came, assuring me when I fretted that things would "turn out all right."

They might, in fact, have turned out a great deal worse. My parents agreed that George could sleep downstairs on the living room couch until he found a job and could afford a place of his own. His presence made it opportune for the whole family to take long, adventurous drives and overnight camping trips in the beautiful San Diego back country. This suited my mother, for she loved above anything else to be on the go and to "see scenery." George did all the work of the camp, which made her feel that at last she had her proper due—she had always faulted her husband for not being "handy" either indoors or out.

Somewhat reluctantly, my father took to George from the start. In a household of females more or less in league against him, the presence of another man must have been a relief. After a few days he remarked that he found George "as easy as an old shoe." Evenings he and George and I played three-handed card games (my mother not caring for cards), mostly, I believe, something called "high, low, jack and the game." In Mexico, some of Papa's boyhood companions had had George's Indian darkness, which he therefore could accept more readily than my mother. To her, any skin not obviously white raised the specter of "miscegenation." It also pleased my father to have someone he could converse with in Spanish, although his dialect and George's were so different that each thought the other spoke very imperfectly.

Even after George got a job as a ditch-digger and a room at the Golden West Hotel, he stll spent weekends with us and, unless the rain was intolerably heavy, our camping trips continued. My mother and father subjected us to a certain amount of petty harrassment, mother coming abruptly into my room in the middle of the night, Papa sometimes making a great display of locking the door at the foot of the staircase. They wanted and at the same time did not want to catch us *in flagrante delicto*. On the road things were not too bad for us. I had my own little tepee tent, the rest of the family slept in a largish striped tent, and George put his bedroll out in the open or under the car if it rained.

The Chevrolet didn't have much life left in it. It had pulled its heart out in the mud of the Missouri bottomlands and shaken its bones to pieces on rugged mountain roads. The time of its demise coincided with my father's receipt of a sum of money from an oil company for an option to explore for oil in his Elm Creek Ranch in Texas. Nothing ever came of the exploration, at least nothing that benefited our family. But he did get enough to buy a big, lumbering Paige touring car. After this we took longer trips. We spent the entire summers of 1921 and 1922 camping out across the country from the Canadian northwest to Texas.

At first mother was careful to make it very clear to everyone that George was not a member of the family. When they shopped for supplies together she would say grandly, "Put everything in one box. The Boy will carry it out to the car," and sweep out of the store well in front of him. What really stung me was the way she belittled him to the girls. Once, for example, we were camped by a particularly large clump of prickly pear. George went over to see if some of the fruit was ripe, referring to them as *"tunas."* Next morning while the younger girl was being dressed—always a leisurely and involved process, and one which only grandmother could attend to properly—I overheard a snatch of conversation. "It sounds silly to call that old cactus 'tuna,'" the child remarked. Then, testingly added, "George talks silly sometimes." Even with her limited linguistic ability, my mother must have known that George had used a Spanish word, but she did not explain. Instead she said severely, "George does talk silly. He's an ignorant, uneducated man." My heart literally burned within me. Just the day before, as we walked down through heavy brush to the shores of Lake Wohlford, this child had put up her arms to be carried, and George had obligingly lifted her to his shoulder. Now to my overwrought thought she and her grandmother conspired in treachery. George was not unaware of these slights and insults, but they hurt me worse than they hurt him. He had the dignity, the humor, and the goodwill to cope with them, and, besides, he was used to the erratic ways of white people.

His patience paid off. Gradually, reluctantly, my mother began to like him, and finally to gain a certain respect for him. She saw a design for a reflector oven in *Sunset* or some magazine of that ilk, and George built it for her. Baking biscuits together in the crisp mornings or canning wild blackberries together by moonlight and firelight in the wilds of Oregon, mother found it impossible to maintain her air of aristocratic superiority. After all, she had never been the southern belle she liked to fancy herself. She had grown up in the bitter aftermath of the civil war. Her family had lost all their meager savings as a result of that conflict, and in their grinding poverty could make no pretense to grandeur.

For a long time after her friendship with George was firmly established she would occasionally lament to me, "If only he wasn't so dark!" But eventually this ceased to concern her. After my father's death she came to lean on George more and more, and after George himself had died, she told people that our marriage had been ideal.

Back in those days of our gypsying, I am sure my mother never admitted to herself that she was exploiting a love affair which she considered sordid to satisfy her own lust for travel and adventure. Yet that is precisely what she did. I, on the other hand, had no delusions and few qualms about taking advantage of her desires, and also of the very real affection which both my parents felt for me.

Perhaps one reason I was such a trial to my parents, and was, in turn, so fearful of them may have been that the difference in our ages was greater than that between most parents and an only child. In large families, there are always children growing up in the home, and older offspring bridge the gap between the parents and those who are late born. But I was conceived after twenty years of childless marriage. Therefore, it was imprinted upon my earliest thoughts that I was something of a freak of nature. The family connections on both sides (none of whom were close, none of whom lived in the same town) referred to me as "the Child," and that is the way my parents spoke of me when I was a bone of contention between them, when they talked at each other above my small and quivering body. I could not, after all those years, have been particularly desired. Yet I am convinced my parents loved me dearly. My mother's love was not altogether pure in motive. Lavishing on me the affection she denied her husband, she could at the same time use me as a shield to ward off unwanted attentions—just as she used my children after me. My father wanted very much to love me, but I had drawn in antagonism with my mother's milk.

Both parents took the matter of my prospective divorce more calmly than I had dared to hope. After all, it was not as if I had been the first woman so to blemish the family reputation. My cousin Irene, after a number of years of supporting herself as an independent spinster, had married a debonair elderly gentleman under the impression that he had money. Unfortunately, he had entertained the same illusion about his bride. In the wake of their mutual disillusionment, Aunt Annie, mother's sister, regretfully wrote us a letter announcing that Irene was in process of "getting a divorce."

My first step toward securing my own legal freedom was to establish residence in California. I tentatively suggested a trip to Nevada. Mother replied with some outrage that a Nevada divorce was not respectable. Me she did not consider respectable, but I had to have a respectable divorce. My father made inquiries and secured the name of a stiff, gray middle-aged lawyer who was reputable and not too expensive. Well before my obligatory year was out, I paid him a visit. He informed me that getting a divorce was not an automatic process and by no means as easy as I had assumed. Desertion would have furnished the most desirable grounds, but that was out. I had deserted my husband. You couldn't just go off and leave a man and then sue him for divorce. I had to admit that I had not written to him since leaving Washington (I don't think I had received a letter from him either, but at this date I can't be sure). The lawyer went into these matters thoroughly at the time and assured me I would have to come up with something better. After all, I must have had a *reason* for leaving him.

Blushing, wretchedly embarrassed, I brought up the matter of sexual deviation, which I had never intended to mention to anyone. The legal gentleman looked very grave indeed. Yes, he said, that was grounds for divorce, but not in this case; I had condoned it. But shouldn't a wife be patient, shouldn't she hope that things would change for the better? Not always; not in this type of situation. However, failure to support our child was a serious matter, even though I had also condoned this by not applying proper pressure. Taking everything into consideration, it was possible after all that I might have a case; but I was made aware of my faults (the worst of which I had not revealed!) and given to understand that my lawyer would really have to work to obtain a favorable verdict. This reinforced my already considerable sense of guilt.

The year expired, I was now a legal resident of the state, and suit was duly instituted about the time we left for our summer's outing. But the lawyer informed us by letter that Harrington could not be located. He was somewhere in the field and proved to be as elusive as a flea. In the event that a certain time elapsed without finding him, it was possible, the lawyer wrote, to give notice by publication in a Washington paper— if Washington was indeed his legal residence. But personal service of the papers was preferable.

What with Harrington's unknown whereabouts (my mother insisted that he was "hiding out on purpose," but this is unlikely) and our peregrinations, the case did not go to court till May, 1922, almost exactly two years after George and I left to drive to California. Harrington came to San Deigo for the hearing. He stayed at his old haunt, the Golden West Hotel, where George still had a room, but it so happened that the two men did not meet.

At this time Harrington did two things, neither of which I understood. (But when did I ever truly understand anything about him?) First, he sent some of my letters to him to my lawyer. I have no idea what they were intended to prove. The lawyer said that, reading them, he "got the impression I knew more about his business than he did." Of course nothing could have been further from the truth. I can only assume that these must have been my letters from Parker; they would have been written with considerable enthusiasm and a certain tone of authority, since I was dealing with a language (and an informant!) as yet unfamiliar to him. As a not excessively well-informed layman, my lawyer was incapable of understanding Harrington's genius and dedication.

His second curious act took place only a few days before the case was to be heard. He requested, through our respective lawyers, that I come down to his hotel room and talk things over privately. My legal adviser and my parents strenuously opposed such a consultation. All three agreed that it was his intention to force me into a sexual act and thereby nullify my prospects of obtaining a divorce. I tried, with a sense of absolute futility, to explain that any typical husbandly behavior, reprehensible or non-reprehensible, would be totally out of character for Harrington. I might as well have been speaking in an unknown tongue. My mother told me I had always been gullible and that I did not in the least understand what men were like. In a snatched moment of privacy, when George and I were doing the dishes together after Saturday night supper, I managed to tell him of the proposition and of my own negative reaction. He alone understood that I had nothing to fear in the way of physical violence, but that I simply could not bear to see the man again, to smell him and to hear his voice, to listen to his recrimination and to attempt to argue the unarguable.

Occasionally throughout the years I have wished that I had over-ruled all objection and overcome my own aversion. I would like to know just what proposal Harrington had intended to make to me in that hotel room. I am sure it would have been some alternative to divorce and complete separation, for in his mind I was inextricably bound up with the work that was his life. At times I have the weird suspicion—almost amounting to intuition—that he might have suggested that he and George and I should go on together just as we had in the past. This is reinforced by a fragmentary memory of something that must have happened in Santa Fé, if it ever happened at all. I seem to remember myself demanding, "Where's George? I want George!" and Harrington's answering, "I'll get him for you," placatingly, as though I had been a fretful child and George my lost teddy bear. Perhaps if I had gone to meet him I would have learned at last if this strange man had enough empathy, enough awareness of other people's emotions, to know that George and I were lovers; or if knowing, he had not cared; or if caring (after his fashion), he had heroically controlled his feeling for what he conceived to be the advancement of his work.

My refusal to ask for alimony or even child support bewildered the lawyer, but he admitted it would probably make it easier to get an uncontested divorce. This man, incidentally, had no inkling of my relationship to George. He knew that I had crossed the continent in his company, but in talking to him, I had deliberately exaggerated George's age and had succeeded in presenting him as an "old and faithful retainer" type. My parents, though they would have liked to have made Harrington pay something towards his child's maintenance, knew better than the lawyer that I was in a precarious position and were quite willing for me not to provoke a dreaded countersuit with its inevitable publicity and scandal. I told them —and they had had enough experience with the man to realize that what I said was true—that he would be stirred up to fight the action if a threat was made against his pocketbook. My own motives were mixed. I dreaded notoriety as much as anyone, but it also accorded with my possibly perverse sense of honor to make no financial demands. That had been my promise to Harrington when I virtually forced him to give me money for the purchase of a car, and it was a promise which I intended to keep.

At that time it was not obligatory in every divorce case for the plaintiff to appear in court. My father appeared for me and was my witness, sparing me a humiliating experience. Harringon was present, closely observing but not protesting the proceedings. He looked unwell and seedy, and blinked his eyes constantly. He did not make a good impression on my lawyer, and apparently not on the judge either. The interlocutory decree was granted.

XIII   Taking The Road
Together

MY FATHER RECEIVED his last option payment from the oil company and bought another new car, a Graham-Paige, which gave us more trouble than its sturdy but now worn out predecessor. When the divorce proceedings were out of the way, we set out to spend our last summer on the road. My father looked forward to our time in "dear old Texas," the rest of us rather dreaded it. This proved to be for me a last return and a farewell to the place of origins.

We went through Coleman and I was able to point

195

out to George the stone house where I had grown up. Then we camped for a few days on Elm Creek Ranch. "Gulf clouds" like gigantic tufts of cotton drifted oppressively low under a sky of hot, metallic blue. The weather was stifling. Only my father was happy—and to a certain extent George and I, because out like this we could always steal some time together, taking walks when the terrain furnished an excuse (which here it didn't) or silently embracing in the dead of night. My father had bought this property with proceeds from the sale of his weekly newspaper and printing office. He had never done any manual labor in his adult life, but loved to picture himself as a country gentleman. There were no cattle on the ranch, which was actually only a few cotton farms and a great deal of vacant land. Papa had three or four tenant farmers. His favorite and head man was "Old Man Markham," who had to sign his name wih an X and could figure only enough to count bales of cotton. My father admired his earthy wisdom.

Next we swung south to visit Aunt Annie on the farm she and two of her sons had bought after Uncle Frank's death. On the way, over my mother's sulky protest, we stopped at Lampasas to see my father's sister, Zona, also widowed. Years had not lessened mother's hatred of Aunt Zona and her brood, but she assumed a surface civility. Aunt Annie told us Cousin Irene was living in San Antonio, and we called on her there in her city apartment. In San Antonio, we stayed in the public campground, which was entirely too public for my love and me.

Last of all, we went to see Tom, my father's youngest half-brother. Papa had a hard time locating him. Tom was not, like other members of his family, moderately successful. It was charitably said that he had been dropped on his head when a baby. He could sign his name, but writing wasn't his forte and most of his siblings had lost track of him. I can't tell precisely in what part of Texas he lived. It was far enough west so that the water was hard with minerals and trees grew only along the watercourses, yet there was enough rain for dry farming. Tom had spent his whole life as a tenant farmer, and no dispossessed Indian ever existed in more dire poverty. I thought this experience should force my mother down off her high horse, but it didn't to any marked degree. She had always tended to look down on my father's branch of the family, even though he and she were second or third cousins.

Tom had "a passel of young'uns" and was living with his third wife. Wives of tenant farmers are apt to die young, but this one seemed pretty durable. She was a big framed, raw-boned, weather-beaten blonde, standing at least a head taller then her husband, illiterate, but good-tempered and a marvelous work horse. With an ethnologist's curiosity, I inquired how she spent her days. She rose at first light, she said, cooked for the family, cared for the little ones, and cleaned up afterwards. Then she took her hoe or cotton sack, according to the season, and went to the fields. If it was cotton-picking time, she dragged her baby along on the sack behind her. She chopped cotton or picked till she judged by the sun that it was time to cook the noonday meal. When that was over, she returned to the field and worked till sundown; then back to prepare another meal and do her housewifely chores. She and Tom had recently lost an eight-year-old daughter. Tom described her as "the cotton pickinest young'un" he had ever known, and mentioned some incredible number of pounds as the child's daily stint. "But," he added piously, "the Lord seen fit to take her." In appearance, as in mentality, Tom was as different as possible from my father. He was short and dark, wiry and compacted from years of toil; he had never read a book, knew nothing about the world outside the Texas farmlands, and his speech was full of strange sayings and odd superstitions.

Only my father accepted Tom's invitation to "come up to the house and set a spell." Mother and I made the excuse that it was cooler down under the trees, and mother would not let her little granddaughters play with the wild country children. My father reported that they had almost nothing to eat in the house, and it was agreed that we should invite them to share our supper. We were camped by a creek that was now reduced to a succession of muddy pools, for it was a season of drought. At supper, Mother, of course, sat in her folding chair, but the rest of us hunkered down on the earth—except Tom's children who, though hungry, were too skittish to come very close. Tom was garrulous. He told how his boys had caught fish with their hands in the mud of the drying pools, and listed all the ailments you could cure with a tea made of chicken droppings. His "old woman" was painfully shy, but she did bring herself to sit on the ground beside us.

On those camping trips, we carried with us a fragment of loosely woven dark green material with yellow and black threads running through it to form a pattern of squares. I don't know what it had been originally—heavy drapery or sleazy carpeting. Now it was worn threadbare, stained and spotted. When we packed, George used it to bundle up the fire-blackened pots and pans, and when we ate, it was spread on the ground to serve as a foundation for a "tablecloth" of clean newspapers. Now sitting silently with downcast head, Uncle Tom's wife spied an edge of this material not covered by newspaper. She fingered it in a dazed way. At last she said remotely, like a woman in a dream, "That 'ere air the purtiest thang I seen in mah whole life. Hit air the purtiest stuff in the world."

It hurts me to remember that apparently none of us even thought of giving her the rag, then and there. But we didn't. In the morning, preparing for a hasty departure, George bundled up the cooking utensils as usual and roped them and the rest of our impedimenta onto the running boards. Even my father was glad to leave that place, and Tom was seldom mentioned thereafter. When our camping-out days were finally over, mother burned the worn-out piece of cloth (or glimpse of paradise, according to one's point of view) in the backyard, where she had burned the clothing I wore when I returned from my first prolonged field trip with Harrington.

George and I reconciled ourselves to waiting the full year, till the divorce became final. Then we would do something, just what we didn't know. But, as I've said, my parents really loved me. Back in California in the fall they talked things over amicably (as they not infrequently did, when the subject was neither money, nor their personal relationship, nor the discipline of children) and agreed upon a wonderfully generous and understanding course of action. My father proposed to cash in the $4,000 insurance policy of which I was the beneficiary and to use the money to purchase a piece of real estate in my name. My mother said, "You want to live in the country. You can buy a little ranch and George can run it for you." She was the one who spotted the advertisement offering for sale "20 acres in Poway," located about twenty miles inland from San Diego.

One blustery day late in October we drove out to inspect the place. A cold dust-laden Santa Ana wind was blowing and our picnic lunch (eaten outdoors on the ground because we wished to talk in private, away from the silent and verbal pressures exerted by the old couple who were so anxious to sell) was well salted with grit. As far as George and I were concerned, we had nothing to discuss. We knew at once that this was our haven and our heaven. The house was, as my parents said, "nothing," an unpainted, two-roomed "California style" shack ("California style" meant straight up-and-down redwood boards with no weather-stripping, and the wind whistling through the cracks). We found out afterwards that it was put together with square, headless nails such as hadn't been used for three-quarters of a century. There was also a rickety, weather-beaten old barn and a small, brand new brooder house, the only well-built structure on the property. But the house afforded shelter and privacy, and we didn't ask for more. The buildings were not what attracted us. The whole place had an atmosphere of age and fruitfulness, something that drew us and welcomed us. The barbed wire of the front fence was strung trunk to trunk on a row of big old evergreens—some sort of cedar, I think, at least that's what we called them. There was a front gate leading to a grape arbor, but everybody drove in the big gate and stopped practically at the back porch. The front yard had been planted with loving care, doubtless by various persons and at various times: a clump of prickly pear by the gate, two gnarled and ancient tea roses, bigger than rose bushes have any right to be; a camphor tree and a perfectly enormous chinaberry tree; and a clump of ragged dark pink chrysanthemums. Another rose, a double Cherokee, whose entwined trunks formed a sizeable tree, spread arbor-like between the house and a cement-floored shed referred to as the "summer kitchen." Besides this shed grew a date tree (which bore imperfect dates because the old man, in a fit of anger at its barrenness, had cut down the male date palm). Back of that was the privy, a two-seater, its entrance modestly screened by redwood boards. Then a few acres of mixed vineyard stretched back to a small sloping field at the foot of a rocky hill on which one granite boulder stood out like a landmark. There was a straggly orchard, a patch of kale for the chickens, and a few chicken pens.

That night George whispered to me, "I didn't say much when we were eating. I was afraid they'd think we wanted it too bad."

The deal dragged out interminably. My father thought the old man was tricky because he refused to leave the tools he had volunteered to throw in, and threatened to back out entirely. But at length, the property came out of escrow. We moved in on the 22nd of January, 1923.

The house was furnished with my parents' cast-offs. Mother said, No, of course I could not take the piano that had been a present to me on my thirteenth birthday, it must be left for the girls; and no, I could not take the good bed that had been bought for me before I married Harrington, the old one stored in the garage was "plenty good enough" for the country; and no, I could not take my demitasse collection, it would just get broken. Nothing dimmed our happiness.

The divorce became final the following May, but George and I weren't married till August. The delay was due solely to my fear of divulging our plans to my mother, a fear which I believe George shared to a lesser degree. The ordeal was not as bad as it might have been. Mother gave a prolonged sniff and said sourly. "Well, if you're determined to go on living with him, I suppose you might as well get married." She also commented that she didn't see how I could stand "to take one man after another." In my mother's book, three men in seven years—as it turned out, three men in a lifetime—added up to promiscuity. However, having spoken her mind, she softened and set to work making me a wedding dress of corded grayish-beige silk ornamented down the front with green beads. (It would be my best dress, in the intervals between pregnancies, for many years to come.) She, my father, and my two little daughters witnessed our marriage ceremony in the office of a justice of the peace, and Mother shed the appropriate tears.

After a few months, when I felt we were settling respectably if somewhat tentatively into the life of the community, I ventured to propose that my children might now make their home with me. It was, I admitted, not much of a place, not nearly what they were accustomed to, but it was a happy home, and the children seemed to enjoy country living. Then it was that my mother put her foot down, as she herself said, "with a vengeance." She also, just as emphatically, "drew the line." She said that if I ever even suggested such a thing again, she would go to court, she would have me declared an unfit mother, she would fix it so that I would never be allowed to see the girls again. On the other hand, if I forgot about this notion, the family would continue to visit at intervals and the children might even stay with me sometimes during vacations. Ninny that I was, and totally convinced of my own unworthiness, I never doubted that she could and would do exactly what she threatened. I was disappointed but not desolated. Now I was carrying my true love's child and had no time for regret.

All this while I continued an intermittent correspondence with Miss Clark. She wished us happiness and expressed no surprise when I wrote her that George and I were married. It must have been through her, for I can't think of any other mutual acquaintance, that I learned, sometime during our first or second year in Poway, that Harrington had learned to drive his own car and that he was doing fieldwork in New Mexico with a female collaborator. The burden on my conscience was somewhat relieved. Now at any rate I knew that by abandoning him, I had not destroyed him. Curiously, I also felt a pang of something quite indefinable—certainly not jealousy, not precisely envy, perhaps more nearly nostalgia, but for life and work as they might have been, not for anything I had actually experienced. I wished for the briefest time that I could have been two persons, leading separate but parallel lives—but neither with the Harrington I had come to know not well, but bitterly.

The happiest years go by and we fail to recognize them for what they are. They are obscured by petty annoyances, present anxieties, or dreams for the future. When I look back upon the years George and I spent together in Poway, I see him in the blaze of autumn sunlight, sweat plastering his blue work shirt to his shoulders, carrying two large wooden baskets filled with the fruits of our earth. One basket might be full of great clusters of Muscat grapes, pale transparent green shading to amber, and the other heaped high with grapes so darkly purple they were almost black; or one basket might hold brown eggs, the other white, laid respectively by Rhode Island Red and Leghorn hens. I see sun-browned children tumbling in the dust beside a row of tall yellow and orange marigolds. I see flowers of all kinds, particularly old-fashioned flowers, and smell the scent of a ragged robin blooming beside the door on a particularly warm Thanksgiving Day, when all the family visited (George drove to town early to fetch them) and my older daughters brought their friends along. I remember the rich odor of food mingled with the fragrance of woodsmoke.

I remember evenings before there were any children, or later, after they were in bed. Many times George and I worked together recording Chemehuevi words and lore, sometimes duplicating what we had previously set down for Harrington, not infrequently dredging new treasures from the well of memory. On other evenings I read aloud and George listened. He liked the novels of Conrad and Hardy, but when I tried to read him Helen Hunt Jackson's *Ramona,* he grew restless, walked up and down, and finally said that the white woman knew nothing about Indians. Of course, later, much later, we spent many evenings listening to the radio, which was for both of us a great and magic door to the outside world.

Then there were the animals: poultry, the goat we puchased when neither canned nor fresh cow's milk agreed with our firstborn daughter, Frances Georgia, and this goat's various descendants; several cows, particularly one elderly black cow (George was sitting under the pear tree milking this cow in the cool, milky haze of late afternoon when the Long Beach earthquake occurred, and later we sat up all night listening to the radio); and the numerous rabbits in the cages George built for them. Besides the utilitarian animals, I remember whole generations of dogs and cats, beginning with a dog named Seaweed, because he had been a ship's mascot, and a spotted tomcat, who brought home one day a slim black bride, so shy she lived up in the Cherokee rosebush for almost a week.

But it wasn't all happy children, sunshine and roses and the fragrance of homemade wine. There were times when even my dreams were haunted by mountains of dirty dishes and soiled diapers. I remember bone-weariness, and poverty so desperate that once or twice I actually scraped the last of the flour from the bin for biscuits, boiled an old bacon rind with garden vegetables for the main dish, and really didn't know where another meal was coming from. Somewhere during these hard years we had to sacrifice ten of our twenty acres to pay off a mortgage we had incurred to finance an ill-advised attempt to raise turkeys. This shocked me profoundly. Since I was a chronic worrier, I envisioned a day when we might find ourselves without any property at all. George loved the land in Poway, even more than I did, but he was inured to the prospect of homelessness and unemployment and refused to be daunted.

If times were particularly hard around Christmas or Easter, I fretted for fear I would not be able to give my children pleasant memories of these holidays, which had been highlights in my own childhood. Of course things always came out right, sometimes at the last moment. One Christmas, being unable to buy a tree and having no money for gas to drive up into the mountains to cut one, George wired together branches from the cedars in our front yard and this is what we decorated. I was no longer so militantly atheistic that I would not put a star on top of the Christmas tree. Indeed, I was ripening towards a religious experience, but it was slow in developing.

When our fourth child was stillborn, I had the traumatic experience of hemorrhaging to the point of death. As I lost consciousness, George whispered, "Don't go!" and I whispered back, with what I thought was my last breath, "You come too." I recovered, but my mind was jarred loose from its accustomed grooves. In front of our house a road ran, and beyond the road lay another vineyard larger than ours stretching back to a farmhouse, then behind the farmhouse a small creek and beyond high hills. Night after night I dreamed that the creek was an impassable dark river, and the hills sky-piercing mountains. There on a peak I would stand watching my home and family, tiny, distinct, inconceivably remote and be unmoved by my husband's grief and children's neglected state. Even awake, I had the sick fancy that the dead child was more real than those who lived. Life went on as usual on the surface. I had another child, born at home on a hot August night after a long pain-filled day. Still my depression did not lift. George had often seen the visible world as possibly a dream-world or alternate reality. Sometimes when we awoke, on those rare mornings when we had a few moments to lie abed and talk, he would say, "I dreamed I was back in Parker and all this had vanished away like a dream" ("vanished" he pronounced "varnished," with an indescribably mournful inflection). He could live with this perception; actually faced by it, I found myself overcome with melancholy.

We were by then fully into the Depression. Hoover closed the banks, including a very insignificant one in Coleman, Texas. My father had helped to found this bank, and in a sense it had been a more satisfactory child to him than his flesh and blood daughter. He survived its closure by just one week, dying quite literally of a broken heart. The night he died we were all together in the home in San Diego. He lay on a hospital bed set up in the alcove off the living room that we called the "music room." My mother sat beside him, holding his limp hand and sighing heavily at intervals, doing her duty to the very end of their life together. The children were upstairs, except the three-months-old baby, who was in her basket in the diningroom, where George and I lay sleepless on a quilt. The folding doors into the living room were partially open. Soon after midnight we heard the death rattle, then the final expiration, and then, no more.

My father died under the impression that all the provision he had made for his family had been swept away. There was no money left except two or three thousand dollars in a joint account in a San Diego bank. The morning after he died I accompanied my mother downtown to make a withdrawal. The account had "dead hand" written across it in red ink. We were at first told that it would remain frozen till the estate was settled, but after some tearful arguments, the bank agreed to release $300 for funeral expenses. Mother stretched it to cover much more. Afterwards, by stubbornly refusing to sign any documents whatsoever or to pay any taxes, she managed to hold onto the San Diego property and Elm Creek Ranch.

We purchased a lot for ten dollars in the unkempt old cemetery at Poway. There on a day of driving November rain we buried my father under the catalpa trees. Mother said this was appropriate, for *his* mother, the mother he had scarcely known, lay under the catalpa trees somewhere near Uvalde, Texas. The gloom of the brief graveside ceremony was broken for an instant when one of the Laird children piped up, "Did we forget the bananas?" To him, the trip to San Diego meant an opportunity to purchase bananas, not the loss of a grandfather.

While he was alive none of us except George had appreciated the head of the family nor given him his just due of affection and respect. Now we all felt the loss of our rock of security. I had not realized that I loved him, yet his death gave a tremendous impetus to the psychic dislocation that had already begun.

My mother was now in a position of needing help rather than being able to give it. George was out of work and I was pregnant again. I drifted further and further into a realm of dreams, then abruptly lost all but tenuous contact with everyday reality. The "nervous breakdown" lasted five months. All the guilts and fears I had repressed since infancy came flooding into consciousness, assuming strange and terrible forms. Such psychiatry as was available to us

(County Hospital type) accomplished nothing. Christian Science brought back the light. Curiously enough—yet perhaps not so curiously, considering the metaphysical nature of Chemehuevi myths and shamanism—its teachings appealed strongly to George. He said, "It's the way I've always worked without knowing it." Contradictory points of dogma, which I had to struggle to make myself believe that I believed, troubled him not at all. He formulated his own calm and generally unverbalized approach to a Supreme Good and to an increased confidence in his own ability.

The Christian Science practitioner whom I had called at the end of my mental illness maintained close contact with the family, and brought everyone around to her way of thinking except Mother, who had no time for such foolishness. She was, she said, "too practical"—and besides she knew perfectly well what was real and what was not real.

Five years after my father's death, Mother's home was about to be sold for taxes. Something had to be done. She received an offer from a firm who wished to purchase Elm Creek Ranch for a fraction of its worth. George and I were opposed to the sale. We felt it went strongly against what my father would have wished—it almost seemed as if we could feel his presence, arguing and contesting against it. The only alternative anyone could think of was for George and me to move back there and run it as best we could with the help of the tenants, trying to make it pay something or, at least, holding onto it till it would fetch a better price. My mother at first favored the plan, then abruptly changed her mind. It had come to her in the night, she said, that this was a wrong course of action. She had had a foresight of all the humiliations and actual dangers we would have to face in Texas because of our racially mixed marriage, and she could not consent to subject us or our children to such an ordeal. Mother was certainly not as a rule a mystical type, but when one of these psychic revelations came to her, there was no shaking her. She went ahead and sold the ranch for a pittance, but it was enough to pay her back taxes and leave something over for her and her girls to live on (wearing odd looking clothes and eating mostly lima beans and cabbage) while they completed their education.

The older girl had not intended to be a teacher. But when she had finished college and still could not find a job, she returned (over her grandmother's outraged protest that she was turning herself into an "oldmaid schoolteacher"), got her credential, and secured a position immediately, even though at that time the supply of poverty-stricken desperate would-be teachers far exceeded the demand. Her sister got a part-time job in the public library. Meantime George had secured steady work on the County roads, so things eased up generally for both segments of the family.

It was, I believe, during this relatively placid period of our lives that we began to have indirect contact with Harrington. He had offered nothing whatsoever towards his daughter's support or education, but eventually, when she had become a young woman, a correspondence sprang up between them. It may have been that our Christian Science friend and mentor encouraged the girl to write to her father—the lady had a good nose for money and wanted her "girlie" to put herself in the way of any possible prosperity. Later still, possibly after they had met, he committed the wonderful typewriter to her care. I know that she had it for a very long time. Harrington had reluctantly learned to drive, but I don't think he ever mastered the art of typing. Through the years George and I had spoken of him only occasionally, to laugh at some amusing episode or to marvel at his strangeness. The animosity I had one time felt had long since been swept away in the floodtide of living

XIV   Beyond The Saddest Time

NEVER BEFORE IN his life had George been inside a church. Now he willingly donated time and effort to renovating the abandoned IOOF hall into a suitable house of worship. This was the joint endeavor of the small group of Christian Scientists in Poway, who had hitherto followed their belief separately and almost in secret. My healing had unified and energized them. Up to this time, the Laird family had not been intimate with any of its neighbors, although the rigors of the Depression had brought us fairly close at times to

209

other residents of the community, mostly newcomers, refugees from the cities. Now we became part of a definite if somewhat eccentric grouping. Despite his friendly disposition, George had always been shy with people, especially if more than two or three were present. Now he took part in business meetings and was not afraid to voice suggestions. Now our children went to Sunday school and were no longer "heathens" —although in the eyes of most of those who lived thereabouts Christian Science was only a step from heathenness.

War and rumors of war inflamed the world. We followed events avidly on our radio. Hitler's raucous tirades reached even into our peaceful community. When actual fighting began, it found me so imbued with what I conceived to be the Christian Science ethic that I felt the mere mention of "retaliation" as a blow upon the heart. Yet I could not help being involved and excited.

I well remember the cold, bright, windy day when we sat clustered about the radio, listening to an account of the pursuit and sinking of the Graf Spee. Absorbed in that far-away drama, George and I sat staring out of the window, absently watching the patch of hard-packed earth where a tiny, lame bantam hen was officiously clucking and scratching for her brood. Shadows of wind-whipped eucalyptus trees (George had planted them as seedlings and they had grown incredibly) played over the busy little family. The hen's feathers were ruffled, the chicks almost blown off their feet. Suddenly a dark shape plummeted down upon them. Quicker than eye could follow, the hen launched herself in a counter attack. We rushed out. A hawk lay on the ground, its neck broken. Not a chick was harmed. Their brave mother clucked more officiously than ever. It seemed an omen, of what we could not say.

Early in April of 1940 our group secured the services of a Christian Science lecturer. Because our church building was very small, we arranged to hold the lecture in the schoolhouse—schoolboards at that time would sometimes consent to such a presentation. It was a tremendous undertaking for a "Reading Group" which had not yet fulfilled the requirements for becoming recognized as a Christian Science Society.

On the Saturday preceding the great event, I went by bus to San Diego to complete some final business arrangements and to consult the practitioner whom we looked upon as our spiritual sponsor. At evening I sat in the station, waiting for the return bus to Poway. The place was jam-packed with bodies, filled with the scent and sound of tense, weary, excited humanity: service men, mostly young; women clinging to boyfriends, husbands and sons; and crying babies. Clearly above the din a voice on the radio was singing, "South of the border, down Mexico way." In an instant, in the twinkling of an eye, my mind was flooded with pure, serene joy. I was aware of everything, I embraced everything, yet I was not saddened by it. I thought of our problems with the children, but was no longer troubled by them. Poignantly, exquisitely, I was aware of George and our home and our life together. That moment in the crowded, littered noisy bus station was the cresting of the wave.

The lecture was scheduled for three o'clock Sunday afternoon. George worked prodigiously preparing for it. He hauled extra seats and put them in place, marked off parking space for cars, and did innumerable chores that no one else would undertake. Our practitioner friend, mentor (and sometimes dictator) had stirred up the interest of her fellow church members, advertisements had been printed in the San Diego, Escondido, and Ramona newspapers, and as a result there was a large attendance. George was the outside usher, directing parking. He wore white trousers and a dark blue coat, hand-me-downs of course (as all our "good" clothing was in those days), but beautifully becoming; and he had a white flower in his buttonhole.

Late that afternoon, after he had finished putting things back in order at the schoolhouse, he was lying on the bed rereading *Science and Health*. I looked over his shoulder and saw that he had reached one of his favorite passages. I commented on this, put my hand on him and asked, "Are you tired out?" He looked up and smiled. "Just my feet," he said. I had never seen such an expression in his eyes before, calm yet bright as flame, kind but immensely remote. I have learned since that such a look is the look of a man who has finished with this world.

Next morning George went to work as usual. It was an intensely bright day, hot for that time of year. I could not settle to anything. I told myself it was a normal reluctance to return to everyday chores, but in fact what troubled me was an overpowering premonition of change and loss. In midafternoon someone phoned that George had had an accident up on the Vallecitas grade. They were taking the ambulance up for him, and I was to await its return by our gate.

He had been working alone in a truck known to have defective brakes. A clod had lodged in the tailgate, he had set the handbrake, and, instead of first getting out and blocking the wheels with stones (which was his normal practice), he climbed back into the bed of the truck to clear it. The brake let go, the truck started to roll. He was thrown out and his left leg was broken in two places. He lay alone for two hours on a sunny mountainslope, loud with bees and fragrant with wild lilac. He mastered the pain, straightened out his leg as best he could, and at intervals called for help. His calls were finally heard by a sort of hermit we knew only as "the Beeman," one of the several lonely mountain people George had befriended.

The ambulance stopped at the gate. Gray-faced but calm, George handed me his worn purse with five dollars in it (all the money we had in the world), smiled and told me not to worry, told the children to do their chores and look out for mama, and agreed that it would be better to be taken to the Escondido hospital because it was closer. The hospital was small and crowded. George received no attention till evening. Unaccustomed to confinement, unable to turn and clear his lungs, he contracted pneumonia and died the following Saturday. The nurse attending him said that at the moment of death his face broke into an expression of "glad surprise."

I felt, perhaps illogically, that he had intentionally lingered till the end of the working week, so that I could receive a full week's sick pay. I needed it, for the insurance the County carried on him did not begin to be paid for three months. It amounted to $68 per month.

I recall vividly a conversation that had taken place between us during the preceding summer. We were limping along towards San Diego in the battered used car which had cost us thirty-five dollars and at that was no bargain. It was the sort of day which occurs not infrequently in the coastal area of Southern California. Hills parched to pale brown rested drearily under a sky of high, uniform gray. A desultory breeze was lifting bits of trash along the side of the road. Feeling the combined effects of drab weather and world tragedy (though as yet without any conscious sense of impending personal tragedy), I remarked, "They say summer is a happy time. I think it's sad."

Somewhat surprisingly, George agreed with me. "Yes," he said, "summer's sad." After a moment's silence, he added almost inaudibly. "But spring's the saddest time of all."

For me, indeed, April of 1940 was the "saddest time of all."

The funeral parlor in Escondido was crowded. Mrs. C., our practitioner, expressed surprise that so many people had turned out to honor "a simple laboring man," even though, as she freely acknowledged, he had been a good man. Besides our church friends and other neighbors, and all the County people (his fellow workers who were given a day off to attend the funeral), there was a whole row of seats filled with strange little old mountain people, wringing their gnarled hands and weeping because Mr. Laird wouldn't be stopping by anymore to fix the pump, or see if they needed an errand done, or just to cheer them with a word. Mrs. C. of course sat with me and the children in the family room. In my bereavement, I needed someone to cling to, and she was more than willing to be that person. After the other mourners had left, after the children had gone out to the waiting car, I stood looking into the casket. But I had only an instant for marveling that in death George looked so sallow, for realizing that his rich coloring had been largely due to the rich blood coursing beneath his skin. My fellow Christian Scientist took me firmly by the arm. "Come on," she said firmly, "George isn't there. It doesn't even look like George." She meant to be helpful. She was living up to the teaching of her religion that "there is no death." I stumbled along with her in one of many acts of somewhat unwilling obedience to what I considered to be superior wisdom and experience. But I could not help thinking distractedly of the "big policeman" in George's song, the one who said, "Come along, you hoodlum, come along."

I can freely forgive this woman for all the snubs and belittlings, for all the times she "ripped me up and down" for the purpose of improving my character—which, like Mother, she considered weak and unstable. I can forgive her for alienating my two older daughters; for persuading me to exercise unduly severe discipline upon my children and George's; and for seeing to it that whatever was salvaged from my father's estate ultimately went to Harrington's daughter, not to me. Doubtless her intervention in our lives actually had very little influence upon the course of events. But I still do not feel that I can forgive her for not allowing me one single moment alone with my dead love, one moment for remembrance, one last moment in which to say "goodbye" and "thank you."

I think it was the summer immediately after we buried George under the flowering catalpas in the plot bought for my father that I saw Harrington again. Or it might have been the following summer. My grief, hidden and repressed, stayed fresh a very long time, and I know that it was still poignant when I went to see the man I had thought never to encounter again.

Harrington was living in a rented house in Santa Ana. He had at long last invited his daughter to spend her vacation with him—or perhaps the girl herself had secured an invitation at the instigation of Mrs. C. My mother (by this time we all called her "grandmother") was old and frail and tearful. She thought it would be advisable for me to go along and size up the situation. Mrs. C. volunteered to drive us. This would give her an opportunity to exercise her infallible knack of judging character.

Harrington's house presented the familiar clutter of neat stacks of manuscripts, dust-covered cardboard cartons, and metal boxes filled with notes. Rows of avocadoes in various stages of greenness, ripeness, and rottenness stood on the windowsills awaiting consumption. The pattern of his life was now irrevocably set. It was certain that he would never learn to understand his fellow human beings, never even superficially adjust to the ways of society. Except for what future students might gain from his publications or salvage from his monumental accumulation of tons of notes, his best talents and insights—and these he had, along with all the weirdness and stupidity—would die with him.

Harrington had, of course, aged but he had not essentially changed. He had grown paunchy, his hair was thinning, and he looked seedier than ever. I had changed more drastically. I was over-weight, had lost several teeth, and child-bearing, physical toil, poverty, illness, anxiety, and the ultimate grief had left their mark. Our meeting was not particularly awkward. Even face to face, I did not loathe him now. If I felt anything at all, aside from resentment of the fact that he still lived and George was dead, it was a very faint pity mixed with superiority, because my life had been so rich and varied and his was obviously running along in the same old rut.

I said, "Hello, how are you?" or something like that, and Harrington responded in kind. He and I had never called each other by our given names. I had not called him John, because this happened also to have been the name of my first lover, whose memory was still green when Harrington and I met. Early in our acquaintance, he had dissected my name and told me that it meant "Dear House." He liked the meaning, but not the name itself because it was a hybrid. The caro-, "dear," commemorating my paternal grandmother, Caroline, was, he said, of Latin origin, while the -beth, "house," after my maternal grandmother, Elizabeth, was from the Hebrew.

(Neither, for that matter, had George ever directly spoken to me by my name. Why, I don't know. Perhaps it was some deeply rooted Indianness which I failed to understand. But George's "you" was profoundly different from Harrington's. George's "primal word" was "I-Thou," Harrington's invariably "I-It.")

In the course of our brief visit, I made some trivial, slightly technical remark on linguistics—comparing a certain Chemehuevi sound to an Arabic consonant, if I remember correctly—and his face lit up with that look of pure delight I had first seen when we discussed my perfect paper in the classroom in Balboa Park. My Christian Science friend and mentor caught and misinterpreted it, even as I had done so long ago. We left father and daughter together and started home. On the way Mrs. C. declared, in the peculiar jargon she affected, that it had been revealed to her that my supply would come through this man. Interpreted this meant: "He is still attracted to you. You can marry him, make a home for him, and in return he will provide for you and your children." I did not argue the point, having long since ceased trying to explain Harrington or the nature of our former relationship to anyone; nor did I say that the last thing Harrington wanted was a woman to tidy up and make things homelike, and the last thing he would tolerate would be the disruption caused by children in the house.

I was, however, sufficiently impressed by the oracular pronouncement to send him the Chemehuevi material I had prepared for publication. This consisted of a series of papers George and I had worked on together. We had "cleaned up" some of the myths and made them suitable for family reading—in those days the public mind equated Indian myths with "animal stories for children," as in a degree it still does, and to these I had added articles on tribal organization, cosmography, and other subjects. After George's death I had appended a glowing tribute to him as a man and as the source of this irreplaceable information. Harrington's daughter typed them all up, with proper phonetic symbols, on the marvelous typewriter. I had not known where to submit this manuscript for publication, and for a while I had not wanted it to fall into Harrington's hands. Now I grasped at the straw that he might be willing to buy it from me or to place it for me. I do not remember whether I sent the articles to him immediately or had his daughter take them to him on a later visit. But send them to him I did, with a letter saying that I had once hoped to publish them myself. Somewhat defiantly, I included everything that I had written about George Laird. Needless to say, I never heard anything further about my manuscript; I ought to have known better than to have sent it.

Shortly after this, both the girls whom my mother had raised stayed with Harrington in Santa Ana for a few days. The older sister was experiencing a weight problem and controlled her figure with a corset. One morning as she struggled into it, she looked up to find Harrington's unwavering gaze fixed upon her. She became incensed, and thereafter tended to regard him as a dirty-minded old man. He wasn't. He was the same old Harrington who had watched with impersonal, scientific curiosity the Mohave woman donning her many skirts.

Years went by. I became estranged from Harrington's daughter for reasons which had nothing whatever to do with him. But, since I had long since lost touch with the somewhat narrow circles in which he was known, the result was that I no longer heard of him even indirectly. I seldom thought of him and had no idea whether he lived or died.

In 1969, I was living in Los Angeles with Georgia Laird Culp, the oldest of the Laird children, and her husband. She had become very active in helping to organize the Chemehuevi tribe and was now in touch with many Indian relatives. We were visited in that year by Stella Smith Mike, of Indian Village, Las Vegas, Nevada. Mrs. Mike, a woman in her seventies, is a daughter of George Laird's half-brother, John Smith; therefore Georgia's cousin, or, in the Chemehuevi idiom, her "older sister." At the beginning of their acquaintance, she had written Georgia mentioning a certain Mrs. Harrington who, if she could be located, would know something about Chemehuevis, because she had come to Parker to learn about them many years ago. Georgia informed her that that woman was her own mother and the widow of Mrs. Mike's favorite uncle. Now it came out in the course of our conversation that Mrs. Mike herself had worked as an informant for Harrington. When was this? I asked. Mrs. Mike remembered distinctly that it was in 1944. He had, of course, been using one of my carefully prepared articles—the one on place names—as his questionnaire, although he had neglected to reveal this detail to Mrs. Mike. What he had said was that she now had the opportunity to complete George Laird's work.

By his time my adrenalin was flowing and I exploded, not altogether in fun. "I told you he was without honor," I said to Georgia, "I'll kill him. If he's alive —and he's probably too mean to die—I'll strangle him with my bare hands." My anger was authentic, though brief. Even though George and I had, by conventional standards, wronged him, it seemed to me despicable that he should use the name of my dead love to ingratiate himself with an informant who happened to be his relative. According to Chemehuevi standards, my outburst was extremely bad mannered: Mrs. Mike looked surprised, but politely refrained from any comment.

Poor Harrington, who had so dreaded death, was already dead at the time of Mrs. Mike's visit. When Catherine Callaghan of Ohio State University visited me in 1971 in pursuance of writing a biographical study of Harrington, she told me he had died in 1961. He must indeed have possessed remarkable stamina to have lived so long in spite of his perilous eating habits and self-neglect. Even after the monumental work of sorting through Harrington's effects, Dr. Callaghan found it difficult to form a mental picture of him as a man. She had come to me in the hope that I might remember anecdotes or incidents which would illuminate his personality.

I was now back in touch with the world to which Harrington by right of his interests and achievements belonged, but from which he deliberately excluded himself. I learned that in his later years, in retirement in Santa Barbara, he had refused to see young linguists who, with the most innocent intentions, wrote him to request interviews. Evidently his paranoia increased with age. About this time I was told by someone that among his great mass of mainly raw notes had been found a small amount of Chemehuevi material, "all ready to go," but for some mysterious reason never published. When I received a xeroxed copy of this, I found that it consisted entirely of the articles I had sent Harrington after our last meeting. On a Serrano-Chemehuevi manuscript he had not even deleted a tribute to George Laird, and my name was included as co-author. All that Harrington had added to any of the manuscripts I sent him was the underlining of words and passages which had particularly aroused his interest.

My interview with Dr. Callaghan forced me to think back to a part of my life that seemed very remote and to recall certain events and emotions long blocked out of consciousness. Having begun to remember, I went on to try to sort my memories out, seeking to analyze them and understand their significance. Then I began to toy with the idea of writing down the little that I could recall of my relationship with Harrington. However, it is hard to write about a very eccentric person without seeming unkind, and I had no wish to be malicious. About this time a friend gave me Theodora Kroeber's biography of her husband. It was so gracious, so lacking in anything even faintly derogatory, that I thought to myself: One should remember the dead in this way or not at all. I almost resolved not to write anything. But in the end it seemed that such a document might not be without human value, particularly if I placed Harrington, whom I understood so little, in contrast with that man who is still more real to me than any living person.

WOMEN OF STRENGTH, PASSION AND BEAUTY... AND THE MEN WHO COULDN'T TAME THEM